THE
SECOND
WIVES
CLUB

THE
SECOND
WIVES
CLUB

Secrets for Becoming
Lovers for Life

LENORE FOGELSON MILLIAN PH.D. *and*
STEPHEN JERRY MILLIAN PH.D.

BEYOND
WORDS
Publishing
I N C

Beyond Words Publishing, Inc.
20827 N.W. Cornell Road, Suite 500
Hillsboro, Oregon 97124-9808
503-531-8700
1-800-284-9673

Editor: Melissa Thompson
Proofreaders: Marvin Moore and David Abel
Design and composition: Susan Shankin
Managing editor: Kathy Matthews

Printed in the United States of America
Distributed to the book trade by Publishers Group West

Library of Congress Cataloging-in-Publication Data
Millian, Lenore Fogelson.
    The second wives club : secrets for becoming lovers for life /
Lenore Fogelson Millian, Stephen Jerry Millian.
    p. cm.
    ISBN 1-58270-014-1 (pbk.)
    1. Remarriage. 2. Wives—Psychology. I. Millian, Stephen Jerry. II. Title.
HQ1018.M55   1999
306.84—dc21   99-31565
                                              CIP

The corporate mission of Beyond Words Publishing, Inc.:
Inspire to Integrity

This book is lovingly dedicated to the jewels in our crown—
daughters Betsy, Nancy, Cynthia, and Melissa—
and their marvelous counterparts—Holme, Sam, and Russ.
Because of them, the design in our lives has been richly
etched with love, with joy, and with glory.

In addition, this dedication embraces our grandchildren,
Alexandra, Jack, Jacqueline, Julia, Zachary, and Samantha,
who have drawn us into their worlds and, in so doing, have helped
us dream the dreams we had forgotten so long ago.

We also dedicate this book to our parents, Florence and Samuel
Fogelson and Celia and Edward Jules Millian. They are
always in our hearts. They provided us with all the essentials
and substantially more. Their love and dedication to each other
and to their children inspired us to realize our dreams.

Contents

Acknowledgments

L O V I N G   A N D   G R A T E F U L
acknowledgment is made to Joel and Leah Fogelson, who with kindness, love, and wisdom guided us toward the completion of this project. Their enthusiasm and support contributed enormously to the realization of our book. Our gratitude and love are eternal. Acknowledgment also is made to that very special patient who inspired the conception of the Second Wives Club group and book with her courage, her love for her family, and her love of God. You know who you are.

This book is also an amalgam of the many individuals who have allowed us to extend a helping hand to them. It is our fervent hope that many others will benefit through reading about the struggles of these courageous people.

Grateful acknowledgment is extended to our wise and patient agent, Jillian Manus; our insightful publishers, Cynthia Black and

Richard Cohn; our resourceful and creative editor, Melissa Thompson; and Kathy Matthews, Cammie Doty, and Pat Maple, all of whom offered sound and needed assistance and advice. Many thanks as well to Robin Miller and Jason Fogelson, who helped budding authors realize their dreams.

Thanks also to the women whose secretarial skills were an essential part of the process of our book. They are Melissa Katz, Nancy Millian, Cynthia Eckhardt, Cindy Heller, and Lisa Slinsky. Lastly, our thanks to proofreader Marvin Moore for his diligence.

Introduction

LONG AGO AND FAR AWAY
in a kingdom called Chicago, and in a state of mind called euphoria,
Prince Steve and Princess Lenore began their lives together. In this
fairy-tale land where bad witches and green trolls were forbidden,
and only good fairies and perfect people resided, the prince and the
princess used the stars in their eyes to guide themselves through
their magical days.

The royal pair dashed about from one corner of the kingdom to
another, spreading their unbounded joy of life to each other and to all
who touched them. By day, Steve and Lenore romped through the
sands of Lake Michigan's shores; by night, only the moon rivaled the
lights in their eyes. After all, they were young; they were in love; they
were invulnerable.

Princess Lenore had married her prince expecting full well to live happily ever after. Why not? That's what the book says—we all know that! She was well aware that her prince had previously married Princess Lily, but Lily had been banished from the prince's heart long ago. Therefore, Princess Lenore did not give this earlier love of Prince Steve's even a thought. The "first" princess was out of the picture and out of the kingdom. Instead, the princess continued to embellish her and the prince's charmed lives by earnestly pursuing her only responsibility—that of polishing her tiara to shine like the North Star.

"Wait," you say—"what's wrong with that picture? To poke holes in that dreamlike, surreal state is to malign motherhood and apple pie! Why can't the kingdom of their highnesses' heaven be forever and forever and forever?"

That image exactly mirrored the young and naïve mind of Princess Lenore, until one day she was awakened by her prince. No, not with a kiss, not with a hug, not even with a handshake. She was thunder-and-lightning-bolted into reality as her husband moaned out the name of his first wife while he came to consciousness from anesthesia after surgery. That moment, the fantasy dissolved and the real world set in. The prince and the princess from the heavenly kingdom crashed down to earth.

The real world, the world in which we both lived, involved one husband and two wives, past and present. Yes, we both thought that this fact was irrelevant and had no bearing on *our* marriage. We did not realize that every event experienced by a person leaves an imprint, a memory trace, an influence. And these experiences impact upon current and future lives. However, they are not to be feared but to be understood. Knowledge is power; ignorance is vulnerability.

In other words, a wise woman must be aware that when she becomes a second wife, she marries much more than just the man. She marries the history with his first wife, his first children, his memories, and so much more.

Over the many years we two have been married, we've become cognizant that it takes work to make our relationship rich and meaningful. Our "second" marriage works because we want it to work (present tense). The adversities thrust upon our union because of its second-wife status seemed overwhelming at times. We persevered.

When I (Lenore) became a therapist years after our marriage, my interest in working with couples having problems due to remarriage intensified. Personal and professional expertise jelled. I developed a passion for working with these couples because of the complexities of the issues and the huge emotional stake involved with the outcome. As time went on, the number of remarried couples in my practice increased, as did the number of remarriages in the United States (approximately 40 percent of all marriages).

Couples' counseling sessions evolved into therapy groups collectively called the Second Wives Club (the Second Husbands Club is in the process of being formed as we write). The "club" groups consist of second wives who meet weekly to discuss their traumas and their triumphs, their conflicts and their resolutions, their loves and their laughs. The club is a safe haven where members find solace and security as they explore their cohesive bond of commonality and link together to find answers. The goals of the group vary according to the individuals, but are underscored by each woman's motivation to get *past* the problems, *past* the anguish, *past* the hurts, and face reality square on to reach the bottom line.

This bottom line is more bankable than dollars, more precious than gold. It is having a friend, a helpmate, a lover in every beautiful sense of the word, for *life!*

Read on, and learn some of the Second Wives Club members' secrets for becoming lifelong lovers. Join the club!

The Nature and Scope of the Problem
(TERRIFIC GUY, TERRIFIC PROBLEMS)

YOU FINALLY MEET A TERRIFIC guy. Maybe you date for a long time, or maybe it happens the minute your eyes meet, but eventually you fall in love, get married, and plan to live happily ever after. You don't care that he was married before. You don't think that it matters—but it does!

Welcome to the world of the Second Wives Club! Membership in the club is open to any of you who experience challenges caused by the fallout from your husband's first marriage. You know who you are! Unfortunately, many times harsh words, arguments, silences, and tears identify you. But the Second Wives Club is designed to change all of these things. Think of the Second Wives Club as a sorority designed to nurture and support you through difficult times. By becoming a member of the Second Wives Club through reading our book, you are eligible to learn secrets designed to help you and your husband become lifelong **LOVERS**.

If you are a second wife, and are experiencing difficulties in your marriage without being able to identify the real issues, this book can help you bring these undercurrents up to the surface. The senior members of the Second Wives Club will show you how to identify your specific problems and needs, and will give you concrete steps to offset these problems. Your behavior is paramount; you may either permit a situation to escalate or you may intervene constructively. You want your relationship to succeed, and this book will show you how.

During the course of the book you will read stories depicting the problems that some of our senior members have experienced—and, thanks to the secrets and support of the club, overcome! Many times, you will find that the problems sound similar to your own. As you read along, try to decide who, or what, is the cause of the relationship problem(s). Remember, the more that you practice this analytical type of thinking, the better you will become at looking at your own difficulties. It might well be that your husband's "first" children or his ex-in-laws provide glitches in your otherwise peaceful relationship with him. Keep in mind that each case is different, and each case is unique. You will learn valuable lessons from other Second Wives Club members. (The material presented in this book is true, but the vignettes represent amalgamations of numerous cases. In addition, the names, ages, and often the genders of the clients have been altered to protect their identities.)

A situation that comes up fairly often in a second marriage is the "three or more in a bed" syndrome. Lovemaking is a very private and intimate part of a marriage. It involves a union solely between a wife and her husband—or does it? At times it might seem as if traces of a third or even a fourth person also are between the sheets—perhaps a former wife or husband is still lingering in the unconscious of the current partners.

Most of us understand that lovemaking is very idiosyncratic and habitual. People have individual preferences in almost everything, whether it be their clothing, dining, or sex. The more we repeatedly act out our unique way of behaving, the more the very act becomes a habit and, as such, takes up residence in our unconscious minds. A couple might fall into a certain sexual routine over the years. This interaction becomes a part of their lovemaking and a part of the way they communicate. In a second marriage, the unconscious memory traces of the former spouse may intrude into the lovemaking within the marriage bed. In other words, the idiosyncrasies and habits of the former spouses manifest as virtually a third or fourth person in bed.

This delicate and sensitive situation can be illustrated in the real-life case of Allison and George. This attractive couple were in their early forties and had been married for eight years when they decided to seek professional counseling. Allison previously had been married to a man who desired to have the back of his neck and ears massaged and kissed as part of the prelude to lovemaking. Allison had enjoyed and accommodated her first husband's desires, and eventually they became a habitual part of the nuances of their intimate life; these acts were enmeshed into an integral part of Allison's unconscious. But Allison soon found that her second husband's repertoire of sexual preferences did not include sensual acts relating to his neck and ears. Although George clearly informed Allison of his discomfort in this area, she occasionally lapsed into her longtime previous behavior of kissing her husband's neck and ears. Allison's former husband was, in effect, the third person in their marriage bed.

George, on the other hand, had been married to a woman who enjoyed playing the aggressor in their love life. George came to accept his first wife's predilections for playing the aggressor and integrated it into his mind as habit, and fifteen years of marriage solidified the sex machinations in George's unconscious. Allison, however, was not used to being the aggressor in a relationship, and did not enjoy the pressure she felt from George to assume this unfamiliar role. Since George had come to accept his previous wife as the aggressor in their physical relationship, he found it difficult to change the pattern; after all, the pattern was acceptable and integrated after many years of repetition. Unconscious thoughts and feelings, by definition, are totally out of our awareness. Moreover, it is believed by mental-health professionals that at least three-fourths of our thoughts and feelings are unconscious. Unfortunately, sensitivity to Allison's needs was sometimes elusive and difficult for George. Wispy traces of this husband's first wife trailed through the bedroom as the fourth person present! This infiltration of the first wife and the first husband into George and Allison's intimate life represented a lingering memory with enormous impact.

––––––––––

DR. M.: It is impressive and says much for the future of your marital relationship that both of you are willing to undergo counseling for your sexual problem. Many people hesitate to discuss this very private subject and are not able to talk about their mutual preferences. Your openness and motivation should result in a successful counseling experience. Where would you like to begin?

ALLISON: As George indicated to you on the telephone last week, we have a very successful, happy marriage. It is our second marriage each, as you know, and we really want to make this work. It works in all areas except one—we can't cover it over any longer, no pun intended! Sex is great, to a point. I've been extremely aware of George's particular needs and desires, and truthfully, I try to please him. I keep in mind that what I've gotten used to over the years may not be to his liking. Occasionally, I forget and George is quick to remind me not to act in a certain way. I try hard.

GEORGE: I appreciate your efforts, but sometimes I feel as though you've forgotten my preferences or that someone else has taken over!

DR. M.: Let's hold the statement that "someone else has taken over" on the back burner for now, because it is going to be very important in our discussion. Allison, can you talk to George directly about what is troubling you about your sex life? I heard that you are trying to please him and trying to accommodate him. Since sex is a very personal and intimate type of communication between two individuals, it is important that George shares your sensitivity. Please speak to him.

ALLISON: George, I've spoken to you before about this. I'm not a prude, but there are certain things that you want me to do in our physical relationship that I don't feel comfortable with. You know what these things are. We've discussed them before, and it hurts me that you persist in your efforts, not every time, but frequently enough to disturb me. [At this point Allison became overwhelmed with emotions and started to cry. Her hurt touched George, who reached over and put his arm around her. She seemed comforted by this, and so we continued.]

DR. M.: I can see that this area of discussion is sensitive and causes pain to both of you. If it continues, it could erode your otherwise beautiful relationship. George, please respond to Allison's comments as if you were in the privacy of your own home.

GEORGE: I understand where you are coming from, Allison. Some of my sexual habits may seem new and unfamiliar to you. They seem to be such a part of me that it is perfectly natural. When I approach you with them, I do so without thinking. I'm very sorry that I've hurt you. I didn't intend to, because you mean everything to me and I love you. But just like I sometimes get the feeling that you don't have control over what seems natural to you sexually, I'm the same way.

DR. M.: OK, George, do you recall that at the beginning of our discussion your statement, "someone else has taken over," was one that I wanted to get back to? This is why! Your former spouse and you had gotten used to each other's sexual preferences over the years. These preferences were unique to both of you—your sexual signatures, as it were. This special way of communicating sexually becomes a habit that establishes itself in your unconscious. It's an unconscious pairing like "motherhood and apple pie" or "black and white." You and Allison are making love, but in each of your unconscious minds you have another reality. Your other reality, George, relates to the sexual habits you formed with your ex-wife, and *your* other reality, Allison, is your unique signature established with your former husband. It surely must feel at times as though a third or fourth person were taking over in your bed. It's important that the two of you understand this concept so that you can gain the power to control it.

ALLISON: I see what you mean, Dr. Millian, when you say that there's a third or fourth person in bed. George, you were right; someone has taken over!

It was clear that Allison and George understood this point, and would make a major effort to integrate into their lovemaking the insights gained in our session. A number of sessions later, they verified that both had been able to make changes in their way of approaching their lovemaking and that these changes were very satisfactory. It was at this time that I introduced the **LOVERS** concept of marital relationships to them:

LOYALTY

OPENNESS

VALUE OF **T**RUST

EMPATHY

RESPECT

STABILITY OF **C**OMMITMENT

LOVERS are the essentials—the foundation—of a marriage. When you and your mate work toward being **LOVERS** every day of your lives, you ensure the permanence of your relationship and marriage.

I emphasized that Allison and George's new sexual regimen would improve the *Value of Trust* component of **LOVERS** which, of course, underscores the *Stability of Commitment* component. The partners said that they would use the **LOVERS** formula as a guide in order to continue to thrive in their marriage.

As you read George and Allison's story, you gained insight into a typical dilemma in which there were not only traces of a former wife present in the relationship but also of a former husband. Each situation is different, and this story is offered only as an incentive to delve into your own conflict. Allison had become a member of the Second Wives Club due to the influence of the first wife on her marriage.

When we become second wives, we marry "for richer, for poorer, in sickness and in health, till death do us part." Based on the annual divorce rate of approximately 50 percent, and a significant second-marriage rate, it might be more realistic to substitute "till your *past marriage* do us part." The rates of divorce and remarriage dictate that hundreds of thousands of women will become second wives by marrying divorced or widowed men.

As a second wife, I am one of you. We second wives live not only with our spouse but with our spouse's marital history. These prior marital histories are far-reaching and potentially can have negative effects on our marriages. As second wives, we have to deal with the fact that "we married more than just the man," and that our husbands have former wives, children, friends, and in-laws, who we must somehow successfully integrate into our lives in a healthy way. However, sometimes when the integration process is underway we experience difficulties that can get out of hand and escalate into crises. As second wives, we are subject to the undetectable, sometimes faint traces of the remains of these first marriages. The intricate webs woven by years of marital history may be both haunting and daunting. Moreover, these problems tend to crop up just when the fledgling relationship is most vulnerable, namely, in the first few years. We will see in the stories throughout *The Second Wives Club* that problems also occur well into the marriage. No second marriage is exempt! According to the National Center for Health Statistics, the average first marriage lasts 6.3 years and the average second marriage lasts 4.5 years. But with the help and support of the Second Wives Club, we can beat these odds by learning secrets to overcome some of the most difficult problems we may face as second wives. We can become LOVERS for life.

Another Second Wives Club story involves Susan and Michael. Susan, forty-two, and Michael, forty-four, had been married less than seven months and considered themselves the "ideal couple." When Michael turned forty-four, his daughter Marcy, from his twenty-three-year-long former marriage, threw him a party, inviting friends, family, and business acquaintances. Michael was unhappy when told that Susan would not be invited, but he voiced no further protest provided the party was kept secret from Susan. Marcy was embittered by the divorce, sided with her mother, and continued to blame Susan for her parents' breakup. Unfortunately, Susan found out about Michael's birthday party two days after its occurrence. She was hurt, enraged, and devastated. These feelings, in turn, led to a major impasse in Susan and Michael's marriage. As a second wife, Susan felt betrayed by Michael's consent to attend his party without her. Michael, on the other hand, told his wife that he was trying to protect her and please his daughter at the same time and he felt that he didn't know where to turn.

This seemingly insoluble problem brought the couple into therapy, where all the dynamics were discussed.

DR. M.: Michael, although you've said repeatedly in our sessions that you love Susan very much, you seem to have a conflict when your daughter is in the picture. It may be that in your first marriage your daughter, Marcy, took an all-important role in your life. This role may have been out of proportion simply because it compensated for a loveless marriage. Marcy was the object of your love and attention for those years of your first marriage. Although she benefited from being the central interest in your life, Marcy also developed a skewed sense of her importance to you.

MICHAEL: But what am I supposed to do about Marcy? Now that I'm married to Susan, I can't just drop her from my life!

DR. M.: Of course not. However, you've said in previous sessions that you fear losing Marcy; she'll be angry with you. You're afraid that if you say "no" to your daughter, she will turn away from you. That type of thinking is similar to giving a three-year-old child candy whenever she wants, for fear that she'll have a temper tantrum. You can be certain that the child will use this very effective tantrum whenever she wants candy. The parent is reinforcing the wrong thing, namely, that a tantrum leads to candy, or negative behavior begets rewards. In your particular instance, I think you can see that *you* are reinforcing negative behavior and setting a very unhealthy precedent. I recall that you told me about Marcy's emotional behavior when you requested that Susan attend your birthday party. When that didn't persuade you to withdraw your request, Marcy refused to speak to you. In your mind, Marcy's alienation was tantamount to a lack of love for you. Therefore, you relented and agreed to keep the party secret from Susan. When Susan eventually found out about the party, she felt betrayed because you compromised her trust in you.

SUSAN: Michael, what I really felt at the time was that Marcy was more important in your life than I was. I felt that I came second to your daughter. I was so hurt!

DR. M.: Michael, you mentioned that you have feelings of guilt because of putting Marcy through the trauma of a divorce. It almost sounds as if you unconsciously feel that Marcy was the wife and not the daughter. I realize that divorce is traumatic for children of all ages, but you divorced your wife, not your daughter. Your daughter will always be your daughter. As an adult, you owe it to yourself to realize the most from life that you can. If this means a divorce, so be it! As an adult in her own right, Marcy has to be helped to come to this realization. Your discussion with Marcy about this issue, along with your appropriate behavior, can be instrumental in bringing about this change. But *your* behavior and attitude must change first.

Eventually, Michael did effect some very powerful changes in his dealings with Marcy. He also spent time with her in discussing their new and more adult relationship. Michael and Susan worked hard to reestablish the bonds of trust and commitment that were missing from their marriage. Our last session was devoted to a reassessment of the marriage, and to the importance of continuing to practice what they had learned in therapy.

It was evident that Michael's divided loyalties toward Susan and Marcy had damaged Susan's trust in him. Once trust is compromised, the foundation of the relationship starts to crumble, much like a weakened house foundation affects the whole house. Susan and Michael took steps to repair and reestablish their trust in each other by keeping the lines of communication always open. They routinely set aside time every evening to discuss the day's activities and any problems they might be encountering. Although the exact time was not written in stone, Susan and Michael found that the commitment to their discussions corresponded to a commitment to each other. Trust is not possible without communication.

As you can see, Susan recognized that the very essence of being a second wife begets difficulties that could tarnish or threaten her marriage. Over time, she and Michael came to understand that a healthy relationship is based on the foundation of **LOVERS**. There is much to be learned from the case of Susan and Michael that you can apply to your own marriage. Always keep in mind that being **LOVERS** ensures that you are enjoying the best relationship possible. It is essential to establish and maintain these qualities. They ultimately provide and encourage an environment in which you and your mate can reach your fullest potential as people. Think of the foundation of a marriage as building blocks. When constructing your house (marriage), you'll lay down the **LOVERS** foundation. Use the foundation to support the first floors, upper floors, and then the roof. A house constructed in this sequence will be strong enough to withstand the adverse elements of the weather (problems). The application of **LOVERS** will create a union capable of withstanding the storms of life.

There are times when a second wife has to assume a strong, protective stance. Such times include potential threats to her marriage by one or more forces, such as a "first" wife, "first" kids, or emotions such as anger and guilt. Such threats to a second wife's relationship must be handled immediately and resolved so that her marriage is secure.

To make this situation clear, we like to compare it to a jack-in-the-box. We all remember these childhood toys that played the "Pop Goes the Weasel" song. At first the music would start out slow and calm, but the more we wound, the faster the music played until *pop!* The jack came out and we would yell with surprise.

Threats to a marriage can be viewed as a "jack-in-the-box" scenario because they, too, have the potential to sneak up and catch us off guard. While going along in our marriages listening to the beautiful music we make together as couples, we must also be aware of the "jacks" that can potentially surprise us at any time. Your mother-in-law, friends of your husband and his first wife, and memories or strong feelings that resurface may act as "jack-in-the-boxes."

Just as when you were a child and knew you had to be aware of the *pop* destined to occur, you need to be aware of the potential challenges that can pop up in your marriage. Be cognizant of the surprise and take action! Our book and the support of the Second Wives Club will guide you through it.

One real-life jack-in-the-box is when your husband is burdened with a deep, overwhelming guilt regarding his former wife and their children. This kind of guilt can be all-consuming and can keep your husband from truly committing to your marriage. Consider the guilt Michael had toward his daughter, Marcy, following his divorce. That guilt drove Michael to do Marcy's bidding and consequently led to a serious marital rift. Is guilt a jack-in-the-box for you? If so, help your husband to recognize and release it.

In chapter 2, we learn that second wives unwittingly may sabotage their relationships due to their own unconscious needs. I call this process "shooting yourself in the foot." In other words, you may not realize that your behavior, which you perceive as "rational," may be quite the opposite. This is nothing to feel badly about; most of our behavior is dictated by such unconscious needs, and learning to recognize and free yourself from these needs will help you to be more responsive, more open, and more clear about what you really want.

What you're ultimately trying to do is to be **LOVERS** in your marriage, every day and in every way, and to make this marriage last "till death do us part."

Chapter 3 is devoted to former wives—a classic example of "marrying more than just the man." The challenges of dealing with a previous wife can really pack a punch in your marriage. This chapter clearly points to the power of a woman no longer active in your husband's lives but still a potential jack-in-the-box! These ex-wives may have seemed harmless at first, but watch out—they may make your efforts to be **LOVERS** for life a bumpy journey.

Children, children—we love them all whether they're babies, adolescents, teens, or fully grown. But let us not forget that your husband's "first" children (vis-à-vis his ex-wife) rank high on his list of priorities. And as such, they evoke deep feelings from your husband, such as fear and guilt as well as love. These very feelings can have emotional tie-ins to the "first" kids and their mother that can sabotage your marital bliss. Check out chapter 4 for a full explanation and remedies for this problem.

The ambiguous role of the grandparents also can become a minefield for you and your husband. After all, the grandparents have not divorced their grandchildren. The importance of these relationships necessitate their remaining healthy and vital to all individuals. However, the jack-in-the-box is waiting to pop! Chapter 5 will help you to identify and to resolve the problems common in these cases.

Chapter 6 details some of the pitfalls confronting the second wife with the involvement of a mother-in-law who may not be pleased about her son's second marriage—another example of "marrying more than just the man." Many mothers-in-law welcome the second wife into their son's life; others present a challenge to the *Empathy* component of **LOVERS**. In which category is *your* mother-in-law?

Still another common relationship behavioral trap is your husband's fear of losing his children's love. This jack-in-the-box may present a challenge in your marriage. Children, whether age three or thirty-three, instinctively use this powerful and manipulative tool. Sometimes this technique is used overtly, for example, "Dad, you hurt Mom's feelings when you left her. I don't want to see you anymore!" Other times the technique is used covertly, for example, when the children forget birthdays, appointments, and so on. The following chapters will help you to identify these types of feelings and their impact on your marriage. We'll help you to spot these problems early and guide you toward their resolution. For example, a jack-in-the-box that is usually not identified is the situation with friends. Your husband's friends from his former marriage may have conflicting loyalties. Are the friends loyal to the ex-wife or to your husband? Do you feel excluded in the conversations about "old times"? Your husband probably wants these people to remain his friends, and is threatened by their potential loss. Chapter 7 fully details the handling of this delicate issue.

Who amongst us hasn't heard a song that brings back a special person or occasion, or experienced a corner of our lives resonating with another time? I call these memories the "ashes of time." Chapter 8 is afire with many and various stimuli that can potentially lead to the disintegration of a marriage. You're certain to benefit from the lessons learned by others.

Chapter 9 is an all-important summary of the highlights of critical points mentioned in the book. Here, some of the important issues of the second wife are reevaluated, as are their resolutions.

Sometimes early warning signs of trouble in a relationship can step right up and smack you in the face, and you shout, "Wow!" Oftentimes, the warning signs are far more subtle. The self-diagnostic quiz in chapter 10 will assist you in evaluating the health of your marriage. It will help you to identify whether you or outside sources (ex-wife, friends, memories, etc.) are causing the problem(s).

Chapter 11 outlines the techniques and procedures for behavioral change touched upon in the preceding chapters. They are delineated so that you may practice them at your leisure and become quite proficient. Use these procedures in conjunction with insights you'll gain from the stories and checklists throughout the book.

As second wives, we must learn to understand the potentially challenging problems inherent in the second-wife status. This book identifies them one by one and brings them to your awareness. It is important to remember that changes can be made only after the source of the problem becomes apparent. On the other hand, if your marriage is progressing smoothly, understanding the potential hazards associated with your husband's first marriage is critical to maintaining your happiness and the health of the partnership. After all, your goal is to make this marriage last "till death do us part"! Let's learn from the stories and challenges presented in this book and discover the secrets of the Second Wives Club, to ensure lifelong marriages for all of us.

––––––––––––

As an assessment of your marriage, please use the next few minutes to take the following self-diagnostic quiz. This easy quiz will assist you in evaluating the LOVERS health of your marriage.

Mark T *for "true" and* F *for "false" on the line before each statement. Remember, be honest in your answers!*
The more truthful you are, the more the quiz can help you.

_____ 1. I feel that my husband has a lot of respect for me.

_____ 2. My husband is totally committed to our marriage.

_____ 3. I feel my that husband doesn't listen to what I have to say.

_____ 4. I am completely committed to my husband and our marriage.

_____ 5. My husband is a very upstanding person.

_____ 6. I want to know everything that's on my husband's mind.

_____ 7. My husband is not very honest with me.

_____ 8. I've never thought that I made a mistake marrying my husband.

_____ 9. Frequently, I'm too angry with my husband to try to understand him.

_____ 10. My husband's first kids are always bothering him— don't they realize that he's got a life?

_____ 11. My husband takes me to restaurants previously frequented by him and his ex-wife.

_____ 12. I usually admire my husband's character.

_____ 13. I have to be careful what I tell my husband.

_____ 14. My husband is always there for me.

_____ 15. I'd back my husband through thick and thin.

_____ 16. I am my husband's priority in life.

_____ 17. I find it scary to be emotionally or physically intimate with a man.

_____ 18. My husband keeps his feelings to himself.

S C O R I N G

LOVERS Positives		LOVERS Negatives

_____ Numbers 14, 15, 16

Marking all three "true" indicates **L**   Marking any of 14, 15, 16 "false"
a long-lasting duo with much   means that you may be questioning
Loyalty.   the values of your marriage and that
(Score one point for each "true.")   *Loyalty* may be an issue.

_____ Numbers 13, 17, 18

Marking all three "false" means **O**   Marking any of 13, 17, 18 "true"
Openness (communication) is great!   tells you that *Openness* (communica-
Be happy!   tion) could be a problem.
(Score one point for each "false.")

_____ Numbers 6, 7, 11

Marking all three "false" means **V**   Marking any of 6, 7, 11 "true"
Validation of Trust is strong   indicates that *Validation of Trust*
in your marriage.   needs work.
(Score one point for each "false.")

_____ Numbers 3, 9, 10

Marking all three "false" means **E**   Marking any of 3, 9, 10 "true"
that *Empathy* is awesome!   indicates that *Empathy* is not a
(Score one point for each "false.")   strong point.

_____ Numbers 1, 5, 12

Marking all three "true" means **R**   Marking any of 1, 5, 12 "false"
that *Respect* is alive and well in   shows that *Respect* may be lacking.
your marriage. Wonderful!
(Score one point for each "true.")

_____ Numbers 2, 4, 8

Marking all three "true" means **S**   Marking any of 2, 4, 8 "false"
that your *Stability of Commitment*   means that your *Stability of*
is perfect! Congratulations!   *Commitment* may be a problem.
(Score one point for each "true.")

_____ Total points (see next page to interpret total score)

INTERPRETATION

16–18   Relationship is very good

13–15   Relationship is only fair but could benefit from counseling

8–12   Relationship is very deficient and needs help

Below 8   Relationship needs immediate help if it's to survive

Encouraging the Problem

(ARE MY NEEDS CREATING THE PROBLEM?)

JANE WAS A SECOND WIFE whose needs created her own problem. Jane had an underlying fear of being deserted by her husband. Most of her past relationships with men had centered on a theme of abandonment. When she was three years old, Jane's father left her mother. Subsequently, he saw Jane only rarely. The pattern of male abandonment was established early on through the loss of Jane's first significant male relationship, her father. Eventually, Jane's mother remarried, and a warm paternal relationship was established between stepfather and Jane. Tragically, years later, the stepfather died in an automobile crash, thus leading to the second male "abandonment" in the young girl's life. The stepfather's death devastated Jane, who had grown to love him deeply as a caring and loving father. Trust became an issue in Jane's future dealings with boys and men due to her unconscious fear of "another" male leaving her. Because of this fear, she lacked the capacity to feel safe and secure with men. Unconsciously, Jane was unable to trust men. She felt that they would leave her—as had the others.

Jane married Jerry when she was thirty-two and he was forty-four. Jane was constantly bothered by her own demons (her unconscious fears and needs), and they subsequently haunted their marriage. This problem was her own. Jerry's love for his wife provided her with the stability, security, and trust that she had missed. Unfortunately, Jerry's business necessitated contact with his former wife. While the contact was legitimate, Jane interpreted it as a situation to fear and a real threat to her marriage. Jane's jealousy, actually stemming from her unconscious fear of abandonment, brought her and Jerry into marital counseling, and Jane sought membership in the Second Wives Club.

JANE: Dr. Millian, I feel so scared that Jerry still loves his ex-wife. After all, she's only twenty-five years old, very pretty, and smart enough to run a business on her own. Why would he love a person like me if she's around?

DR. M.: Jerry married you for many reasons, but most of all because he loves you and you are very special to him. Jerry has shown you this love in so many ways. I wonder why it is that you do not believe him. Any ideas on this?

JANE: I know that you're quite right, but I have this feeling of doubt in Jerry and can't believe that he actually loves me and wants to stay with me. Then, when he sees his ex, my distrust in him is overwhelming and I become totally undone.

DR. M.: Jane, is there a past relationship you've had with a man that had been ongoing and happy before Jerry came into your life?

JANE: Actually, if I think about it, any relationship I've had in the past has been short-lived. The guys always broke off with me, sometimes without an explanation.

DR. M.: In other words, Jane, time after time you've been left by men, emotionally torn apart and abandoned. This began with your father and then your stepfather. No wonder you've not been able to trust Jerry. You've unconsciously felt that he, too, would leave you. You were trying to protect yourself from further hurt. Understandably, you had to back away from Jerry. In other words, Jane, your need to guard yourself against the further pain of being deserted by yet another male in your life was founded in your unconscious fear of being abandoned by men. This fear truly was a creation of your own, and it was born out of your *need* to feel loved and secure. An unsettled fear from the past is a type of demon that haunts you from your (or someone else's) past actions. Your needs are your own demons. As we progress in therapy, you'll be able to put these unsettled fears behind you, where they will be harmless. The element of trust in a relationship is vital and cannot develop and flourish until your fear is dissolved.

Jerry and Jane both attended counseling sessions, during which time the concept of being **LOVERS** in a relationship was introduced. All of the components of **LOVERS** were introduced to the couple, particularly that of *Value of Trust*. Simultaneously, a number of behavioral skills helped Jane to get in touch with her irrational rages and to bring her back to the reality of Jerry's love and their marriage.

One of these important skills, Thought Stopping (see chapter 11), is very effective in helping individuals stop destructive behavior quickly. This technique may be added easily to your repertoire of helpful skills, as an aid to reduce the impact of negative thoughts and behavior.

As counseling progressed, Jane became aware of her unconscious fears and needs and their damage to her relationship with Jerry. Eventually, she and Jerry were able to remain **LOVERS** for life. Jane was finally a practicing member of the Second Wives Club.

As illustrated in the preceding case, Jane's needs and fears encouraged her marital woes. As a second wife, this chapter may be critical to you in learning how to recognize your unconscious needs, so that they won't play a part in your marital relationship. You may inadvertently and unconsciously encourage or promote problems relating to your second-wife status. As human beings, second wives have certain needs that must be satisfied. It is said that most of these needs are unconscious and stem from childhood. Despite all conscious efforts to change your way of behaving, you may have noted that you've become "stuck in a rut." This "quicksand" hold on you originates from your needs. Until you become aware of these needs, they will continue to sabotage your intent to make changes. Remember, your goal is to remain **LOVERS** for life, and to not allow unsettled fears of any nature to mar your relationship. To assist you in getting in touch with your own needs, please review the following statements taken directly from real-life situations. The fears that are hidden in the context of each statement will prod you to delve into your own thoughts and needs. Suffice it to say the number of needs that individuals have is infinite! So, consider these statements merely as examples:

He's my husband and his only responsibility is to me!
Unconscious thought: I had to share my parents with siblings, but I won't share my husband! (Emotional immaturity)

If my husband has contact with his former wife, he might go back to her!
Unconscious thought: Other women have more value than I do! (Insecurity)

I don't want their children to visit my husband in my house!
Unconscious thought: Messy rooms reflect badly on me! (Need to be perfect)

Our kids and theirs should not see each other!
Unconscious thought: My father's favorite child was my sister! (Jealousy/rejection)

My primary role in life is keeping my husband and our children happy!
Unconscious thought: I always tried to please my parents so they'd love me! (Low self-esteem)

All photos of their marriage should be destroyed!
Unconscious thought: My family moved eight times when I was a child and I always had to make new friends! (Insecurity)

Please take time to complete the following quiz, to determine if problems in your marriage are triggered by your unconscious needs. Constructive methods for change are outlined in a checklist following the quiz.

Q U I Z

Mark T for "true" and F for "false" on the line before each
statement. There's no sense in bending the truth!
Mark the first answer that comes to mind. Remember, your feelings
are valid and can be used as a learning tool.

_____   1. I have not had a good relationship with my father.

_____   2. I've often felt that something is missing from my life.

_____   3. My parents fought a lot.

_____   4. I find it very difficult to be loyal to one man only.

_____   5. I feel that having sex with my husband is an obligation.

_____   6. I feel that my husband has had regrets about marrying me.

_____   7. I've often wondered why my husband married me when he knew lots of smarter and more attractive women.

_____   8. The more my husband goes out of his way to please me, the angrier I become.

If you have marked a "T" beside any of the items in the quiz, be aware that your possibly unrealistic and unhealthy needs may be instigating, contributing to, or perpetuating a problem in your marriage. Insightful information is provided in the following checklist. Are *you* the jack waiting to pop out of the box?

---

1. A healthy relationship with your father is a good barometer of your future relationships with men. After all, your father was the first significant male in your life. You might want to examine your situation carefully to determine the influence of this critical and powerful relationship. Should your father–daughter relationship be weak or inadequate, either work toward improving it or accept it as such. Try writing a letter to your father expressing your feelings. Don't mail the letter, but use it to clarify your feelings and to release any anger you may have toward your father. Forgiveness is essential.

2. Women often make the mistake of using the men in their lives as instruments of completion; that is, having a man makes them feel whole and complete. If your life is somewhat empty and you feel unfulfilled, ask yourself if you are using your husband to add excitement and stimulation. Do you feel incomplete as a person on your own, without borrowing from your husband's identity? If so, this is an unhealthy need and a real "jack-in-the-box" surprise of your own creation.

3. Your parents' relationship becomes the role model for your relationships. In other words, the way that your parents relate to one another becomes the template in your unconscious for the way men and women actually *are*. If the main features of your parents' marriage were conflict, hostility, and anger, you might well have internalized such features into *your* way of being in a relationship. Please think about this item carefully, as sometimes it is difficult to be objective about your parents.

4. If you find that your eye—or more—is wandering, you might want to explore the reasons behind this meandering. Possibly this has occurred because your marital sexual relationship is unsatisfactory or uninteresting. Simply put, you may be bored with it. Another reason for a wandering eye could be that you fear putting your trust into one man alone because of the hurts that you've suffered in the past. Review your past sexual history. Have men cheated on you at one time or another and more than once? Consider the *Value of Trust* and the *Loyalty* components of LOVERS in light of your history. Is your unconscious need to keep yourself safe from hurt becoming the recurring problem in your marriage?

5. If you feel that having sex is an obligation, there are many avenues to explore. Examine your private life with your husband to assess its quality. Had it been rich and rewarding at one time? If your sexual activity once captured your heart but no longer does, think about the good times and when those good times fizzled. Was there one pivotal moment or situation in which your interest diminished, or was it gradual over time? These are important considerations!

Take a moment to ask yourself about the degree of sexual attraction or "chemistry" that you felt for your husband. Was this attraction weak or strong in the beginning? A rather low degree of attraction between individuals logically results in a low degree of sexual happiness. On the other hand, if this attraction had been strong, question the possibility that other interests are taking over your conjugal bliss. You also might consider speaking to your physician in order to rule out any medical problem responsible for low libido.

No matter the reasons for your lack of sexual desire, take note of the feelings that you experience when "obligated" to perform an act for which you have no interest. Your inner demons in this area could be the cause of the problem. It's hard to remain LOVERS for life when sex is a problem.

6. Unless your husband actually has expressed regrets in marrying you, it would be wise to consider other sources for your feelings. Some of these sources might stem from negative self-statements such as "Who wants me anyway? I'm a loser. I don't seem to matter to him." The value that you place upon yourself (your self-esteem) may be an important factor if you feel your husband is unhappy that he married you. Sometimes we are very much aware of our low self-esteem, and other times we are not. Either way, low self-esteem leads to insecurity in a relationship and to nasty and troubling feelings of jealously and envy. Are these problems preventing you from becoming a successful member of the Second Wives Club?

7. This statement also addresses the issue of self-esteem, but additionally it encompasses the concept of self-confidence. One who has a healthy confidence level does not care about who is smarter or who is more attractive. It just doesn't matter! If you find that you constantly are comparing yourself to others—either favorably or unfavorably—you may be shooting yourself in the foot! Your need to seek approval from others is rooted in your need to give yourself a boost to help

increase self-confidence. Make a list of all your wonderful aspects, carry the list around with you, and review it daily. It is important to remember that confidence springs from accomplishments. Look into yours!

8. If you responded "true" to this statement about feeling angry the more your husband tries to please you, take the time to explore your feelings very carefully. When your husband's efforts to make you happy breed anger within you, there's a problem. Possibly the problem may be that, unconsciously, you have trouble respecting that he puts your needs before his. Some might interpret selflessness as weakness. Or, your anger might be an expression of underlying distrust of men in general. Consequently, your husband's efforts to please you play into that distrust. The stronger your husband's efforts, the angrier you become. Try to become aware of your unconscious needs so that you can eventually dispel their strong hold on you. Hostility and anger lead to a powerful double whammy when trying to remain LOVERS for life!

Self-esteem issues arise repeatedly in my practice and seem to play a very pervasive role in relationship problems. One reason for the prominence of the self-esteem issue is that it negates the *Respect* component of LOVERS. Unhealthy self-esteem leads to a lack of self-respect. And it is well documented that if you don't respect yourself, your partner won't respect you as well. By the same token, strong self-esteem leads to strong self-respect on all counts.

One of the many couples who illustrate this particular difficulty is Lois and Henry, twenty-four and twenty-eight, respectively. Both of these previously married clients came into counseling because they were choosing to spend more and more time apart in order to avoid conflict. They said that they loved each other but felt lonely and isolated within the marriage. The distraught couple had been married for seven years and had no children.

In our initial meeting, it was apparent that both Lois's and Henry's levels of self-esteem and self-respect were quite low. Consequently, each did not appear to respect the other's choice of marital partner, believing that "You couldn't be so wonderful if you chose *me* for your mate!" In other words, these partners were unable to be LOVERS because the mutual respect that is so critical in a marriage was missing.

I urged Lois and Henry to start individual counseling for a limited period of time, until couples therapy could be effective. In that fashion, each person's self-esteem could be strengthened prior to working as a team. I emphasized that each person must bring individual strengths to the relationship to build a strong foundation for a marriage. The elements of LOVERS were discussed continuously with this couple, so that the entire concept could be woven into their joint therapy sessions.

Since this book addresses wives, only the sessions with Lois will be used to illustrate the ways in which a second wife unconsciously can encourage and, indeed, even create a problem in a marriage. Until this problem can be corrected, such a wife cannot successfully be a practicing member of the Second Wives Club!

Lois had married her childhood sweetheart, Tony, the day after graduation from high school. She had declared that Tony was "the love of her life" and that at age eighteen she was mature enough to know what she was doing. Lois said that she remembered being anxious to get out of her parents' home because of feeling unwanted and unloved. Lois felt that her parents had been overly critical of her almost constantly, oftentimes humiliating her in front of others. Children raised in such an environment do not develop the positive feelings about themselves that are necessary for healthy self-esteem and self-respect. Such children seem to identify themselves as losers and make their way through the world with a negative mental outlook. They feel that a black cloud follows them throughout life.

DR. M.: Lois, now that you can look back on your first marriage, can you see how your relationship with your parents affected your decision to marry at such a young age?

LOIS: All I wanted, Dr. Millian, was to have someone special in my life to love me, and I thought that Tony was that someone special. Now I can see that I had to leave my parents' home for my own survival. I didn't think that anyone else besides Tony would want me, and I really wondered why he did!

DR. M.: Unfortunately, your home life was such that you grew up lacking healthy self-esteem and looked for someone else to provide it. How long did this marriage last?

LOIS: Well, Tony lost his job and we had to move back in with my parents. After that, things went downhill, and Tony became as critical of me as my mother and father had been. We stayed together for about eleven months, and then I asked him to leave.

DR. M.: That truly was a difficult situation, and it required courage on your part to end the marriage. When did you meet Harry?

LOIS: I met Harry a few months after separating from Tony. I actually thought that he was the answer to my prayers because he treated me so well. We got married a few months after our first meeting.

DR. M.: It would seem that you married Tony to escape from your parents' wrath and that you married Harry because of his kindness to you. The underlying theme here seems to be that you married in both instances in order to feel good about yourself, since it is quite evident that your self-esteem was fragile. How sad that you needed to look to others in order to acquire a healthy identity! You cannot relive the time in your childhood when your parents should have been helping you to grow emotionally strong. But becoming aware of the dynamics of the situation is the first step to getting beyond it and then to gaining a healthy sense of your own identity, which is crucial for a successful relationship.

Over a period of time, Lois came to realize that much of the difficulty and turmoil she had encountered in her marriage was due to her low self-esteem. Her self-confidence grew as she came to grips with her life. Behavioral techniques helped Lois attain a positive sense of herself. Harry's individual sessions were productive as well, and the stage was set for their relationship to come into focus in joint counseling sessions. The work the couple had done individually provided an important foundation, because relationships based on need (regardless of the need) cannot result in a healthy marriage. Both Lois and Harry came to recognize that healthy self-esteem equals healthy mutual respect. Establishing the *Respect* component of **LOVERS** actually reinforced the *Stability* component and consequently led to a warmer and more soul-satisfying marriage.

Another unconscious and quite powerful need that all too frequently rears its ugly head in discordant marriages is the need to be in control, a need that strikes a very familiar bell with many women. The need to be in control, actually, may emanate from feelings of insecurity. After all, if you have all your little ducks lined up just so, if you know where your mate is at all times, if you hold reign over the only family checkbook, you then have a substantive sense of security. This unconscious need sets off a powerful series of dynamics in a relationship that may erode its very essence. Let's see if the following story rings true for you. If it does, it is wise to become aware of the fact that your need to be at the helm may encourage jack-in-the-box scenarios.

Madeline, age fifty-six, and Zachary, age fifty-two, had been married for almost twenty-five years. The divorce from his first wife devastated Zachary. He was desolate. Then he met Madeline. His new love owned a rather prominent boutique that she had started with a modest inheritance. Madeline used a good deal of her energy to succeed in the business, and she had prospered. She was relieved and pleased that Zachary had agreed to do the bookkeeping for the boutique.

Madeline was proud of herself, and rightfully so. Both parents had died when she was very young. An elderly aunt and uncle were the only family members willing to take in the ten-year-old orphan. Three years later, both relatives passed away within a short period of time of one another. Madeline was then placed in a state institution, where she remained until reaching the age of majority.

The couple had no children—the boutique was their child. Madeline ran the business with an iron fist and took charge of every aspect except for the bookkeeping. She controlled the buying, the selling, the salespeople, and the bookkeeper! She also controlled all aspects of their home life, and this pervasive control had led to many arguments over the years. Zachary had tolerated the situation for the sake of the business.

When she became fifty-five, Madeline sold the business, thereby thrusting Zachary and her into a new aspect of their relationship. Madeline no longer had a business to control, but her personality trait still required her to retain control. Now the entire focus of the day centered on her husband. She transferred her need to control the business to a need to control her home and her husband.

Her control fostered an enormous stress, to the extent that Zachary's blood pressure soared. He finally approached Madeline with the strong suggestion that they see a marriage counselor. Zachary was truly unhappy being the object of Madeline's need to control every aspect of life as they lived it. At first, Madeline balked at the idea of seeing a counselor, but relented when she realized that Zachary was desperately unhappy and that it was out of character for him to be uttering any kind of protest.

DR. M.: Madeline, during the initial session when both you and Zachary spoke jointly to me, I noticed that it was you who did most of the talking. You certainly are an articulate person, but I wonder if your husband also has something to say about your situation. He had initiated the counseling sessions but seemed to be reticent to speak. What do you think?

MADELINE: Zachary is a quiet man with not much to say. That's why when he started complaining about our relationship, I listened. I hadn't realized that he was so unhappy.

DR. M.: At our joint session, Zachary said that he actually had been unhappy for a long time but hadn't been aware of it. Perhaps your husband's unhappiness had been covered over by the demands of your business and the pressure both of you were under in running such an enterprise. But now, with time on your hands, your relationship has come into focus.

MADELINE: Exactly! All these years Zach was willing to follow my instructions about running the boutique, and because I was the boss, he was compliant. He seemed happy to have an important role in the business and never forgot that I gave him the job.

DR. M.: It almost sounds as if you're angry with Zachary. "I gave him the job" is a strong statement.

MADELINE: I suppose you're right. He didn't complain about our relationship when the business was active and he needed me. Now things are different. Also, he continuously refers to Anna, his ex, who as you know is a well-known stage actress, talented and beautiful. She left him—I didn't!

DR. M.: But while you were in business, Zach's references to Anna didn't bother you. So many things change when a person retires. The dynamics of a relationship are such that when the basic situation changes, the dynamics change. Let's try to zero in on the problems that brought you here, namely, Zachary's contention that he has no "room to breathe" at home. He feels "smothered." From the many examples he gave during the joint session, would you agree that there is validity to his complaint?

MADELINE: Sure, I can see that. But don't forget that Zach didn't have a way of making a living until he married me. He had been jilted by Anna and seemed lost in life. I gave him a start and gave him a life.

He looked to me to make all the decisions—so I did! I know that when I make a decision, it's well thought-out and most of the time right on the mark. I learned to depend on myself. Zach had trouble with decision-making and leaned on me for everything.

DR. M.: Madeline, given your background in which you lost your parents and your aunt and uncle very early in life, we can understand why you were compelled to develop a strong sense of independence. You learned that you cannot rely on anyone in this world—because those on whom you did rely passed away. Unfortunately, you acted as your parent. More than likely, a child in that situation develops two feelings simultaneously, namely, a sense of power and a sense of insecurity—power, because of feeling independent, and insecurity, because of being bereft of loving and caring relatives and being placed in a state institution.

MADELINE: But what has that to do with my marriage? I brought my strength and independence to the table, and both worked well for all these years. It worked well for Zach, too—we were able to retire early.

DR. M.: This is all true. It is impressive that you did so much with your life when you had such a shaky start. In a large sense, your success had to do with your insecurity, because you must have discovered early on that you had to control the different factions in your life in order to feel secure. In other words, your need to feel safe, secure, and powerful had to be based on your own ability to provide yourself with those same feelings. You learned to trust only yourself, to rely upon only yourself. Control was a critical factor in your daily functioning. Can you see that your basic survival skills, which stood you in good stead in business, actually backfired for your marital relationship? Your need to control Zachary should be viewed as an ongoing continuation of the way that you learned to function in this world. However, you're no longer the vulnerable child or the insecure young woman. Let's talk about this again in future sessions and see if it doesn't make sense to you.

Over a period of time, Madeline came to understand clearly how she had encouraged problems in the marriage and had created her own jack-in-the-box. The problem in the relationship was not due to Zachary's ex-wife but manifested by Madeline's own unconscious need for control.

In the aforementioned cases, the unconscious needs of the second wives were hindering and preventing successful memberships in the Second Wives Club. Their motivations to feel safe in their respective relationships led to behavior that was destructive for themselves. But not everyone feels abandoned, not everyone feels insecure, and not everyone has low self-esteem. Please examine your own background and explore your own inner needs. Remember that the present (here and now) recapitulates the past (what once was). You may need the services of a professional to help you along, and that's OK! The important issue here is to be objective in your role as a second wife so that you and your mate can obtain *Loyalty, Openness, Value of Trust, Empathy, Respect,* and *Stability of Commitment* in your marriage. In other words, you both should work toward being **LOVERS** in a warm and loving relationship. Good luck! You can do it with the help of the Second Wives Club!

Challenge Number One: The First Wife
(OR, HOW TO EXORCISE A GHOST)

MOST OF YOU HAVE MARRIED with the best of intentions and the highest of expectations. Although fully aware of your husband's prior marriage, you assumed that he was "over it" and that *it* was "gone," as if he were cured from a dreaded cancer. However, you may have noticed increasingly that lingering traces of your spouse's former marriage creep into your life and intrude upon your relationship. This intrusion may be vague and indefinable at first, but over time it can become a major challenge in your relationship. This chapter explores the warning signs of wife number one's presence, and what that presence means to you and your marriage. The purpose of this section is to help you recognize the subtle beginnings of difficulties stemming from the memory of the first wife, and what to do about them.

As you read through the following story about one of our Second Wives Club members, it would be helpful to get in touch with your emotions, to imagine yourself in a similar situation. Do be kind to yourself, and realize that people change very slowly over time. We take only baby steps, not giant steps. And the first major step you can take to make a change in your relationship is to make the decision to do so! Congratulate yourself for that! Your second step to make a change is to become aware of the problem. Your awareness may or may not be hidden within the stories, but real-life examples will get you thinking in the right direction.

Caroline and Jack, a couple in their early thirties, were very content with one another and their marriage. But only one month after their wedding, the challenges began for them in the form of crank telephone calls, intercepted mail, and surprise confrontations by Jack's ex-wife, Molly. Although Molly's behavior certainly was deplorable and aggressive, Jack's reactions were those of pity, fear, and anger. He felt pity for Molly that she was hurt and rejected; he felt fear that her irrational behavior might well result in a nervous breakdown; and he felt anger that Molly's behavior might cause dire stress in Caroline. In his efforts to put an end to Molly's intrusions, Jack frequently called his ex-wife begging her to cease her behavior. In so doing, Jack fell into a trap by maintaining a relationship with Molly. Furthermore, Molly in her hurt and rage felt empowered by Jack's responses and continued to fuel the fire with her annoying and sometimes frightening actions. These mini-traumas escalated into a major rift in Caroline and Jack's marriage. Caroline felt that her marriage had been violated and was threatened. She was alarmed over Molly's power to control Jack and was disappointed in his handling of the matter.

Naturally, this led Caroline to question Jack's feelings toward Molly and toward herself. She began to question Jack's loyalty to her.

JACK: Dr. Millian, do you have any idea of how guilty I feel for pulling out on my wife the night I left her? The facts are that our marriage hadn't been going well for years; we constantly argued. Our discussions ended in screaming matches. We had sex six times in our five years together. Nonetheless, when I left her I felt tremendous guilt. Perhaps I should have stayed; she's wiped out from this. What kind of man can I be to destroy another person's life and completely change her style of living?

DR. M.: Of course, you wouldn't purposely cause another's unhappiness, Jack. However, all the years that you were married, you caused your own unhappiness. You cannot purposely cause another's unhappiness. You are a person also, and your staying with Molly led to your unhappiness. Doesn't that count at all?

JACK: Truthfully, I never thought about it that way. I am so used to always thinking about others—that's how I was brought up. Everyone's happiness came before mine. In my household, if I thought of myself, my parents would call me selfish—especially my father.

DR. M.: There is a phrase that I like to use occasionally: "enlightened selfishness." The use of the phrase does not advocate extreme selfishness, namely, taking advantage of others. Enlightened selfishness simply means taking good care of yourself and fulfilling *your* needs.

JACK: It doesn't sound as if I did that in the marriage at all or in my life. No wonder I was unhappy.

DR. M.: Let's face it, Jack: you said that throughout your life you've concentrated on helping others. Partly, this philosophy might be due to your religious upbringing and/or to your family. You've even become a social worker to help people, but how long can you continuously give out "goodies" without getting some "goodies" back? After a while, you run dry—you burn out. And then you can't help anyone.

JACK: It's too bad Molly doesn't feel the same way. Over the years, she wanted much more from me, and was so angry and hurt that I had to leave. Now it seems as if she's taking all sorts of extreme measures to get back at me—I call it harassment. Her behavior isn't normal! I'm really afraid that she's working herself into a nervous breakdown, and the guilt would be overwhelming if she had a breakdown and I caused it!

DR. M.: Jack, you don't have the power to cause a breakdown in another person; only Molly is able to do that to herself. Molly's responsibility is to take care of herself and her mental and physical health. Likewise, Jack, your responsibility is to do the same for yourself. Your first major step toward that end was to leave Molly. You told me that she refused to go to counseling although you repeatedly expressed your discontent in the marriage. She ignored your pleas, and ignored your feelings. What choice did you have but to leave Molly and start a new life for yourself?

JACK: I understand what you're trying to tell me, Dr. Millian, and I appreciate your insight. Because of my guilty feelings, I almost sacrificed Caroline and our marriage. This has put Caroline under tremendous stress. Why, she's even asked me if I love her or love Molly!

DR. M.: Do you recall that in the joint session with Caroline, I spoke to both of you about my concept of a healthy marriage, using the acronym **LOVERS**? Your ambivalence about Molly put your marriage at risk because Caroline's trust in you was wavering—and without the *Value of Trust* you cannot have *Stability of Commitment* in your relationship. Furthermore, Caroline questioned your love and *Loyalty* to her. You really should keep the **LOVERS** concept in mind as you and Caroline take the necessary steps to repair your marriage.

In further sessions, Jack recognized that his angry responses to Molly's provocative behavior provided her with much satisfaction and also helped Molly to maintain a connection to him. Jack was also helped to understand that the pity and fear that he experienced was, in reality, part of the guilt he suffered for his rejection of Molly. All of these insights were of direct assistance to Jack in working through the guilt and eventually relinquishing it. Jack's new realizations and insights into his unconscious were powerful tools in dislodging the power of Molly's relentless and dangerous behavior. In Jack and Caroline's scenario, the traces of the first wife nearly severed an otherwise healthy, budding marriage.

At this point, you may be wondering if your husband's first wife has been your entrée to the challenges in your marriage and the obstacle preventing you from becoming a successful member of the Second Wives Club. Yes, she's a pain in the neck. Her phone calls sometimes seem excessive, but is she really a challenge in your marriage? The following quiz might just prod you into some serious insight about your situation.

Mark T for "true" and F for "false."
Your first answer is your most heartfelt and honest.

_____ 1. Although reality tells me that only my husband and I share our bed, I sometimes feel as though traces of his first wife are present.

_____ 2. On my birthday, the gifts that my husband buys for me consistently are not to my taste (for example, floral perfume, pink lingerie, and vanilla candy). I'm happy that he thinks of me, but I can't help but wonder if he confuses her preferences with mine.

_____ 3. My husband's ex seems to call at dinnertime with problems concerning "their" children. I sometimes think that my husband is afraid to ask her to call after dinner because he doesn't want to upset her. I almost believe that he'd prefer to upset me.

_____ 4. It sometimes seems as if our lovemaking is tainted by another's preferences. I wonder if my husband's sex with his former wife influences our sex life.

_____ 5. My husband makes blatant reference to his ex-wife's culinary skills.

_____ 6. Even if my husband's former wife uses strong-arm tactics, he won't give in to her if her demands are unreasonable.

_____ 7. My husband always acknowledges his ex-wife's birthday with flowers.

_____ 8. My husband's ex-wife does not keep in contact with him at all.

C H E C K L I S T

1. If you answered "true," it would be a good idea to examine the *Openness* component of **LOVERS**. Communication between you and your husband in this area is critical, and if you sense that wispy traces of his ex-wife are floating through your sheets (as in the case of George and Allison in chapter 1), it might be timely to discuss this issue. Three (or more) in a bed prevents your success in the Second Wives Club as you journey toward becoming **LOVERS** for life. Make sure this isn't the case with you!

2. His remembering your birthday—and your remembering his—is a given in any relationship. After all, a birthday is a special event, and it is made even more special for the remembering. If you responded to this statement with "true," it may well be that the other woman who had shared his life preferred a floral-scented perfume or pink lingerie or vanilla candy. It's possible that this is just one clue that your spouse's ex is a jack-in-the-box waiting to pop!

3. If you answered "true," it would seem that your husband might be sacrificing your needs to his former wife's needs. Here's where the *Loyalty* component of **LOVERS** comes in! You'd better discuss this calmly with your husband before it escalates.

4. If you answered "true," perhaps the lingering memory of your spouse's first wife is in *his* head. Lovemaking has to have elements of *Value of Trust, Empathy,* and *Openness* to be fulfilling. You should take the necessary steps to speak to your mate about your sexual preferences and your feelings. He might not be fully aware of them. But keep in mind that it is always a good idea to praise a person before you offer any constructive suggestions. Keep talking and you'll surely get rid of this jack-in-the-box!

5. If your husband comments on his ex-wife's culinary skills and this is a frequent occurrence, it is likely that the former wife's presence is in your pots, cabinets, and kitchen. Since this is an area of concern to you, let your husband know that you feel hurt/angry/annoyed/disappointed (pick your own honest feeling). When he praises his former wife's cooking, let him know that it feels like a put-down to you. Underneath it all, your feelings may be nudging you to wonder why his ex-wife is still on his mind and in his stomach. That woman's kitchen skills may be a jack-in-the-box waiting to pop!

6. If you responded "true," isn't it great that your husband's ex does not intimidate him? Be certain to tell your mate how good it feels that he doesn't let this woman push his buttons. On the other hand, if you answered "false," meaning that your husband tends to feel threatened by his ex, gently point this out to him and talk about it. His first obligation is to you, despite her threats or demands.

7. Your husband's act of remembrance of his ex-wife's birthday causes you to question every element of **LOVERS** because it is tantamount to being unfaithful emotionally. Your husband is aggressively encouraging the presence of his former wife in your marriage by sustaining an interest in her birthday. You seriously might want to consider marital counseling in the near future. Your feelings of *Value of Trust, Love,* and *Loyalty* are being compromised when your mate maintains a connection with someone important to him in his past. If your spouse doesn't cease and desist, the effectiveness of your membership in the Second Wives Club will be compromised.

8. If your husband's ex-wife never contacts him, obviously there is no indication of a lingering presence from her. Consider yourself fortunate!

The comments in the checklist above should serve as a prod to determine the existence of a problem in your marriage that might be attributable to your husband's first wife. Sometimes, the difficulties emerge in a very subtle, almost indiscernible, way. The intention of the quiz is to help you detect small problems so that you might qualify for membership in the Second Wives Club.

Although there are a great many warning signs that could be construed as wife number one's lingering presence, there is another common situation that is exemplified best in the next real-life story of a Second Wives Club member. In this example, you will see how Michelle was in need of the secrets available to Second Wives Club members.

Michelle had been married for three years to Robert. Both of them were twenty-eight years old, and prided themselves in their wisdom and maturity in knowing each other more than eighteen months before marrying. This was Michelle's first marriage and Robert's second. They appeared to have tremendous respect for one another, both personally and professionally. He was an electrical engineer, and she was a professional chef of some renown. On the surface, the couple seemed to get along well, but underneath it all, there were rumblings of another kind. Michelle's area of professional expertise was food, and she felt that the kitchen was her purview. She was occupied with food preparation both in a restaurant and in the kitchen at home. Michelle's strength was in the creation of exquisite and unique meals. Her weakness lay in her organizational skills. Robert was devoted to Michelle and had no complaints about their marriage except in the one area of her "sloppy" work habits. He couldn't understand how she could continue to work successfully given her apparent disorganization. It was apparent that Robert's engineering brain functioned on a different level than that of his wife's. His talent was in his focused, methodical, orderly system of analyzing, evaluating, and thinking things through. Michelle's talent was the polarized opposite. Her brain was energized by the myriad of stimuli impinging on it, and these stimuli were the very sparks of her creativity. Michelle feared that if she became outwardly organized, as Robert desired, she might lose her expansive, artistic capabilities. She felt that her artistic prowess could be compromised if she tried a more controlled, deliberate way of working. In others words, although she admitted that at times she could not locate the "right" pot or the correct ingredient in her kitchen, Michelle was contented with her approach to assembling meals of gourmand quality.

Further complications became apparent as my discussions with Robert continued.

ROBERT: There's something else that I haven't said to Michelle, Dr. Millian, and this is that I don't like my food elevated to the degree of art which Michelle seems to feel it must be. I don't like the fancy meals that she makes, and when I offer to cook, she turns me down flat with tears in her eyes.

DR. M.: It's obvious that you're used to eating very simply and that you feel uncomfortable with the lavish meals that Michelle concocts. Tell me, was this a problem in your first marriage as well?

ROBERT: Absolutely not! Tonya and I took turns cooking, but we both prepared simple meals with simple ingredients. Tonya knew how I felt about food. I want plain food, not some crazy, artsy combination arranged on a plate like a piece of sculpture.

DR. M.: I can't understand why you haven't informed Michelle of your preferences. She seems to be under the impression that you object to her lack of organizational skills, not the kinds of meals she makes.

ROBERT: I haven't the heart to tell her. When I cooked, I prepared simple dishes, and when Michelle asked me how I acquired my basic cooking skills, I was truthful in saying that Tonya taught me. That happened lots of times, and more and more it seemed to stick in her craw. It really bothered her that I was using Tonya's cooking methods and not even trying hers. Michelle used to say that it was like there was someone else in the kitchen besides her and me.

DR. M.: So, because Michelle resented your rejection of her style of cooking in favor of Tonya's and you feared setting up the two women in "competition," you developed another strategy of showing annoyance with her organizational skills. It appears to be your way of getting back at Michelle for not paying attention to your needs and at least making an effort to please you gastronomically.

ROBERT: That's exactly right. I can't help but feel that if Michelle really loved me as much as she claims, she'd be more receptive to my likes and dislikes. Other areas of our marriage are great—but this one is a major problem. Maybe if she didn't cook so fancy, she'd have the time to organize the kitchen the way Tonya and I liked to live.

DR. M.: It almost seems as though you are saying that you need to have perfection in your marriage so that you can be happy. Perfection occurs in heaven but not here on earth with people. Perhaps what you are really saying is that when Michelle doesn't consider your wishes 100 percent, she is in effect rejecting you as a person. You might want to think about that statement carefully and see if it doesn't have special meaning to you. Your former wife's food preferences just happened to coincide with yours. Michelle's do not agree with yours—but should that be an issue?

ROBERT: Are you trying to say, Dr. Millian, that I'm being unreasonable with Michelle? I feel that I'm just trying to help her get organized in the kitchen. She could be in and out of the kitchen in less time if she were more organized. What's wrong with that?

DR. M.: Please understand, Robert, that there's no right or wrong way to work in the kitchen. It has to do with the way in which Michelle feels she can work best for herself. Let's consider these thoughts. First, if Michelle's efficiency improved, you feel that she could reduce the time spent in the kitchen. Second, if Michelle prepared meals simply and more to your liking, it would also get her out of the kitchen faster and have the added bonus of pleasing your palate. In both instances, Michelle would be able to give you a lot more attention than she does now. You two would have more time together. And how special you'd feel if she adjusted her style of cooking to your preference!

ROBERT: Dr. Millian, I think you've hit upon something I didn't want to face, and this is that I really don't feel very special to Michelle at all times. After all, she has a successful career that consumes a lot of her time. More time is eaten up away from me when Michelle cooks fancy in a haphazard kitchen. Both the disorganization and the elaborate meals are unnecessary and excessive. I believe in economy of time and effort, and she doesn't. I think I feel deep down that if I were truly important to Michelle, she would do things my way.

In time, Robert realized that the underlying motivation in his urging to have Michelle change her culinary habits was unrealistic. Further sessions helped Robert work out his need to feel special in every single aspect of his married life. Once he truly understood the needs that underscored his motivation, Robert was able to get past them. In addition to these insights, Robert was encouraged to use stress-management skills (see chapter 11) so that he'd have more patience with Michelle.

Joint sessions with both Michelle and Robert focused on the components of **LOVERS** on which they needed to concentrate, including *Openness* (their communication skills were inadequate), *Value of Trust, Love* (Robert's trust in Michelle's love for him had weakened), *Empathy* (Robert was encouraged to be more understanding of his wife's weak organizational skills), and concomitantly the fragile *Stability* of their marriage.

The presence of Tonya, Robert's first wife, loitered in the couple's kitchen only in his unconscious. Nonetheless, the apparition hovered over Robert and Michelle in such a way as to challenge the strength of their marriage. For Michelle, the intrusion was a metaphor for Robert's excessive need to feel special in her eyes.

Robert's need became a powerful force in disrupting the marital relationship. It also hindered Michelle's successful membership in the Second Wives Club! However, once Michelle and Robert learned the secrets of becoming LOVERS for life, Michelle was able to become a successful practicing member of the club.

As a second wife, it would be helpful for you to note how Michelle and Robert scored on the LOVERS scale. It will give you good practice when it comes to your evaluation of your own score. How would *you* fare?

Still another scenario comes up all too frequently: Your husband's divorce is final, his former wife is but a memory to him, and yet he finds himself face-to-face with her—again and again! Where do these "rendezvous" happen? Not on a street corner, not at a hotel or a restaurant, but in a court of law! "Does it ever end?" you wonder. No! There goes your spouse—in court once more and in turmoil once more. The lingering presence of the first wife hits you both right smack between the eyes—vis-à-vis legal motions, inquiries, and more money out the window and into the attorneys' pockets. It is irrelevant whether or not your husband's first wife's court dates are appropriate or necessary. They may well be. No matter what, using the legal system to resolve matters in marriage ranks as the number one factor in wreaking havoc upon marriage number two. The next couple present a typical case in which just such a situation occurred.

Nicole and Ed had been married for eighteen months when he was summoned to court by his former wife, following custody problems they had been unable to resolve. Delays and postponements triggered one anxiety-laden month after another. The apprehension of the possible impact of the court decision coupled with a huge financial outlay resulted in a tumultuous six months for Nicole and Ed. What had been a carefree and satisfying marriage now became one of strain and stress. The couple struggled to get back to the loving environment that had once been theirs, but instead they found themselves on shaky ground. Prior to the final court date, Ed and Nicole sought couple's counseling.

DR. M.: From what you have told me in the initial consultation, the two of you have enjoyed good times together. Your marriage had been going well, and you appear to have been devoted to one another. You obviously *want* to continue this marriage but want it to be nurturing and happy as it had been in the past. Can you bring me up to date and tell me what precipitated your need to call me?

NICOLE: Yes, what you've said is true. Ed and I have had a wonderful relationship and our first year was like heaven on earth. You couldn't find a couple happier than we were. Ed meant everything in the world to me. I was OK with the former wife, but . . . it ended on a bad note, according to Ed.

ED: If I could interrupt for a minute, I want to say that Nicole is right on target. Things were great between us, and I only wish that I had met her earlier and married her in the first place. What a mistake it was to marry Peggy!

DR. M.: It seems as if you both had everything going for you. You had love, loyalty, and trust in one another, and from what you said last week, you spoke openly and honestly. What happened?

NICOLE: The court date happened. The delays happened. The postponements happened. The not knowing what was occurring with Ed's kids happened. The money out the window happened.

DR. M.: You sound angry, Nicole. Your replies have an edge to them. Why the anger?

ED: That's what I'd like to know. This business wasn't my doing. I tried to negotiate with Peggy, but she wouldn't budge! I called her; I met with her face-to-face—nothing worked. It was Peggy who got us into court and drained our money. I didn't want to give Peggy what she wanted—after all, the kids are mine too. And I should have a say in the way they're raised.

NICOLE: Yeah, that's true. But it wasn't *my* doing!

DR. M.: Nicole, anger can wear a person down. It depletes energy and erupts into stress. How do you feel about Ed's attempts to negotiate with Peggy? Can you talk about them?

NICOLE: Sure, Dr. Millian, I'm angry—no, I'm *furious* at Ed. I don't think it's really a big deal to give Peggy what she wants. She wanted to give Ed no choice in which weekends he got with the kids; she wanted to have the only option over that because she said that she was the one raising them. She wasn't trying to take the kids away from Ed, but she wanted the visits at her convenience only. In my mind, that's not so terrible. And if Ed had agreed to it, we wouldn't have had the agony and expense of legal and court fees. It's breaking the bank!

ED: It's breaking the bank—and it's breaking us! It's put us into a situation where the tension is like a tightrope wire. We argue over anything and everything. It's turned our marriage upside down. Nicole, I'm hurt that you can't understand why I won't give up my rights to the kids.

NICOLE: You wouldn't be giving up your rights to the kids—only when you could see them. You're being unfair!

In subsequent sessions with the couple, Nicole talked about the poverty in which she grew up. Her mother raised her and her three sisters alone. The father had a debilitating illness. Having little money and living a life without basic necessities had a profound effect upon Nicole. She and Ed had reached a place in their lives where they were comfortable and could enjoy the nice things in life that were far from her grasp in her earlier years. The current situation in which she and Ed found themselves acted as a painful trigger to the deprivation Nicole had suffered. As a child, she feared that she might not survive. As an adult, Nicole saw the world through the eyes of herself as a child—somewhat skewed and distorted.

Through the next sessions, Nicole was helped to understand the paradox in which she existed: the present financial situation had recreated the terror under which she had lived as a child. The paradox overshadowed her concern for Ed and his rights to see his children at mutually predetermined times. When Nicole realized the power of her unconscious in contributing to fallacious reasoning, she was able to relent. She was also able to give up her anger and to see that it was really a case of displaced anger targeted for her childhood. Although Nicole's parents were blameless and had worked hard to provide for their large family, Nicole's anger was a child's anger and very real.

Both Nicole and Ed were taught the Progressive Muscle Relaxation Exercise (see chapter 11), so that they could learn to handle the stress of the court sessions and the decision of the court. The many valuable components of LOVERS were discussed with the couple in order to give them an understanding of a healthy marriage's foundation. Which of the aspects of LOVERS do *you* think were emphasized in the case of Ed and Nicole? This story should be a valuable tool from which you can learn about yourself and your relationship!

All three of the foregoing stories are but the "tip of the iceberg" of the infinite possibilities of warning signs that traces of your spouse's first wife have infiltrated your relationship. Again, they are offered in order to stimulate your thinking in this particular area. Has the trace of the former wife become a jack-in-the-box for you? How can you, as a second wife, best deal with the challenging presence of wife number one? Taking a cue from the second wives in this chapter, as well as learning from checklists and the vital information in chapter 11, should help *you* become a successful member of the Second Wives Club.

Challenge Number Two: The Children
(THE "FIRST" CHILDREN, OR "THEIR" CHILDREN)

BRUCE AND OLIVIA WERE IN
their mid-thirties and had been married for over five years. Bruce's
twin sons from his previous marriage were active in many sports and
participated in competitive games regularly. Bruce's divorce had
been brought about largely as a consequence of his former addiction
to alcohol. Bruce realized that his alcohol problem had deprived his
sons of "quality" fathering and felt that the divorce compounded the
deprivation. In order to appease his overwhelming guilt, Bruce made
certain not to miss a practice or a game in which his sons played.
This determination of Bruce's to overcompensate and be the "attentive and devoted" father led to many absences from Olivia and their
young children. Tension mounted after each game, leading to a serious rift between Olivia and Bruce. They tried to resolve their differences on their own, but it seemed that the paternal situation in which

the couple found themselves was like a minefield inviting destruction. At this point, Olivia called for an appointment for both of them.

DR. M.: From my understanding of your situation, it would appear that the two of you have been able to work out other problems that have come up in your marriage but you're stymied with this one. It is in your favor that you've expressed your determination to get your marriage on a positive course. You've declared quite openly that you love one another and trust one another implicitly. All of these factors bode well for a positive outcome for your marital counseling sessions. Please give me some insight into the difficulties you've been experiencing with regard to your sons, Bruce.

BRUCE: Well, Dr. Millian, in my twenties, I was quite a drinker. I didn't see it as a problem because I never missed a day of work. In fact, I got an award from my company for the employee with the longest-standing record of work attendance. So, I thought I was doing OK! I never considered myself an alcoholic. I thought that alcoholics were drunks who couldn't keep a job.

DR. M.: What line of work are you in, Bruce?

BRUCE: I drive a truck—but I never drove it if I had a drink. I drank after work and on weekends only. I provided a home and food and clothing to my wife and boys and thought that was it. That's what I was supposed to do—be the breadwinner. When my wife started coming down on me for the drinking, I went to the bars at night. She covered for me and told the kids, "Daddy's working at night, too." They were little guys then, and by the time I got home or was carried in by my drinking pals, they were asleep. My wife was mad at me all the time, and this went on for over six years. For a while she bought beer for me so that I wouldn't leave her at night. She made it so easy for me to keep drinking—and I did see the boys more. But now I know that a drunken father is like no father at all. Cathy finally told me that she couldn't put up with my drinking anymore and that she'd leave if I didn't get help.

DR. M.: It's interesting that Cathy saw you as a person with a drinking problem but made it easier for you to drink by having beer in the house. She acted in what we call a "codependent" way. It sounds as though Cathy tried the "if you can't lick them, join them" strategy, and when that didn't work, she tried the more desperate measure of giving you an ultimatum.

BRUCE: I was angrier than hell! Who did she think she was to threaten me with kicking me out? But she did! It happened during a weekend that I was drinking. I was drunk; I pushed her; she called the police and got a restraining order; and that was the beginning of the end!

OLIVIA: But you've got to tell Dr. Millian, Bruce, that you've not missed an Alcoholics Anonymous meeting for six years and you've not touched a drink for that long. I'm real proud of you!

BRUCE: Thanks, Olivia. I'm proud of myself, too. But now that I'm sober, I realize that I've missed so many years of my twins growing up. They're nine years old already. What kind of a dad have they had? Same kind I had, I guess! The boys are terrific in sports; they play soccer, basketball, and baseball. I *want* to be there for them; I *need* to be there for them. Why should I miss a single practice or a single game? They look up at the stands and see their dad there. Dr. Millian, I'm finally able to be a *real* dad to them—not just a father.

OLIVIA: And that's the problem. Every spring, fall, and winter, at least three or four times a week, there seems to be a practice or a game. I can't go with Bruce because I don't want to run into Cathy. So, he's away from me and our kids so much of the time.

DR. M.: It would seem, Bruce, that history is repeating itself in that you're missing your and Olivia's children growing up. Has this crossed your mind?

BRUCE: Yeah, but they're so little that they don't know the difference—one's a newborn and the other is fourteen months. I gotta be with my boys!

OLIVIA: What about me? Don't I count, too? I *am* your wife. Why do I have to compete with your twins for your time and attention? It just isn't fair!

It was apparent that Olivia was questioning Bruce's priorities and his loyalties. Because of Bruce's ambivalence on the loyalty issue, the marriage was becoming unstable. Two very vital components of LOVERS were being compromised: *Loyalty* and *Stability of Commitment*. Olivia had not just one jack-in-the-box waiting to pop but two in the form of Bruce's sons. These jack-in-the-boxes were not due to the twin's initiative but to Bruce's. As you read how Bruce slowly became aware of his underlying motivations for setting this up, it would be a good idea for you to explore possible explanations. As you do, you will gain insight into yourself as well. Learning about others gives you a more objective view of unhealthy behaviors and their impact on marriages. Which component(s) of LOVERS is (are) most relevant for you?

DR. M.: It is quite commendable that you are addressing your alcohol problems. I know what an effort it must be for you. It's also commendable that you now want to be the best father you can to your twins, because of not being there for them all those years. Can you talk about the feelings that motivate you to attend all your sons' practices and games?

BRUCE: Sure. "Guilt, guilt, guilt." How can I possibly make it up to them for not being a good father? The only way I know is what I'm doing now. What's wrong with that? I love Olivia and our kids, but I feel awful about my boys.

DR. M.: I think that something else is going on here that may be keeping you from developing a clear understanding of your behavior and attitude toward your twins. We've agreed that guilt is the driving force motivating you to take an extreme course of action in being with the twins so frequently. However, in addition to the guilt, let's think about the possibility of another reason for your excessiveness. You see, the more you know about what makes you tick, the more you can change things. Bruce, we've established that your former alcoholism and the consequent absences from home led to your feeling that you've been a less-than-adequate father. Because of this, isn't it likely that you are plagued with feelings of insecurity as a father and now wonder if the boys really love you?

BRUCE: Sure. Why wouldn't I feel that way? Why should they love me? I've been a terrible father to them.

DR. M.: The boys love you because you're their father, and although you've admitted to being a negligent father in the past, you're there for them now. You seem to be afraid of losing them, and because your fear is powered by guilt, you go to the extreme. As much as you may try, you can't make up the time lost by *overdoing* now. And in the interim, your young children need you as well. Can you see that you are sacrificing both your kids and your marriage because of trying to overcompensate for your guilt with the twins? And that guilt is fueling the flames with insecurity and fear.

Throughout the counseling sessions that followed, Olivia was encouraged to develop more empathy toward her husband's trauma, and Bruce was helped to come to terms with his guilt and his fears. Furthermore, he was able to achieve a balance in his relationship with his sons in a healthy and constructive manner. The challenge of Bruce's children ("their" children) soon dissipated because Bruce was no longer energized by guilt. Thereafter, the marriage prospered in a positive direction. Bruce and Olivia were led through the LOVERS concept of a healthy marital relationship, with an emphasis on *Stability of Commitment, Loyalty,* and *Empathy.*

This chapter explores common father–child scenarios involving an insecure, guilt-ridden parent and children who, perhaps inadvertently, exploit that weakness. The scenarios are, of course, different for each second wife, and are intended only as aids to uncover the problem underlying your individual set of conflicts. "Their" children can prevent you from becoming a successful member of the Second Wives Club. Have the first children challenged your membership?

The following quiz will help you assess your husband's "first" children's impact on your marriage. Be sure to read and to evaluate the important points regarding potentially unhealthy situations. They will assist you in determining if "their" kids present challenges in *your* marriage.

Q U I Z

Mark T *for "true" and* F *for "false." Remember, again, that your first response is generally your most truthful response.*

_____ 1. I am not included in activities that pertain to "their" children.

_____ 2. My husband spends an excessive amount of time with "his" kids.

_____ 3. Most of the money I earn at my job goes to "their" children's support.

_____ 4. Our vacations are infrequent, and they always include "his" kids.

_____ 5. My husband's children speak to me disrespectfully.

_____ 6. I am so pleased that my spouse has a close relationship with his kids.

_____ 7. I know for a fact that "his" kids carry tales from our house back to that of their mother.

_____ 8. My husband's child insists on sleeping in bed with us when he visits.

1. If you're not included in the activities of "their" children, please look into the reasons behind your being overlooked. Not being invited could be a signal that you're not being recognized as an important new member of the family. To "their" children, you might well represent the "real" reason for the divorce ("If it weren't for you, Dad and Mom would get back together again"). Children unfailingly *always* want their parents to reunite—no matter how much these same parents argued. It's quite possible that you, as a second wife, are being blamed by the kids for keeping their parents apart. This thinking is not based on reality—but when you're a child, reality sometimes is shaky. Despite the reasons for not being included in their kids' events, it is to your credit that you recognize it as a problem. Taking steps to correct this problem would be right in line with your efforts to confront the challenge "their" kids may present. Talk to your spouse about your feelings—and then invite the kids into your discussion. Acknowledge their feelings, tell them you understand, and encourage them to talk openly to you and their dad.

2. Look into your heart to define what you truly believe is an "excessive" amount of time. Do "his" children take 10 percent, 25 percent, or 40 percent or more of your husband's available time? If the time your spouse spends with his kids is unreasonable, given your circumstances, discuss it with him. Should you answer "true" to this statement, you might want to help evaluate his motives. As in the case of Bruce in

the previous story, perhaps guilt is the underlying factor in your husband's desire to be with "his" children for an inordinate amount of time. Helping your spouse to look into his motives can offer him valuable insight into his behavior. "Don't play psychologist with me" might be his response to your offer to help. Should this be the case, suggest calling a professional. Remember, the second component of LOVERS is *Openness*. It's a good idea to strive toward open communication between you and your spouse, but also realize that he may not be ready to hear certain insights of which you're aware (after all—*you're* reading this book, not he). Backing away in order to move forward is sound strategy; a counseling situation allows you to do this. It also may bring you one step closer to mastering the secrets of the Second Wives Club!

3. Unfortunately, a lot of second wives answer "true" to this statement about having to support "their" children. It is a fact that the average divorced couple has less in the till than when they married. The parental responsibilities of your husband do not end, of course, upon remarriage. It is likely that your spouse's financial responsibility to support "his" children is a drain on the resources of your current joint marital pockets. A second wife often finds that child support is dependent on a second income—hers! Yes, the presence of "their" kids meanders in the shadows of your checking account. However, please remember the children's innocence in the scheme of things. It may be difficult for you *not* to build up resentment toward them or toward your husband. It might be a good idea for you

to set aside some small portion of your income for yourself in order to offset your negative feelings in this case.

4. "False" would be the answer of choice as to whether or not your vacations are infrequent, but most likely "true" is more on target. Typically, time, money, and vacation are at a premium; there's just so must of each to go around. From a realistic point of view, that's just the way it is. However, from an emotional perspective, the lack of special vacation time with your husband can lead to enormous feelings of anger and resentment on your part. You might want to consider the possibility of having to accept that vacations, for the time being, do include his children and perhaps yours. Think about making weekends away with your spouse during the year as an acceptable and pleasant way of vacationing. It is not ideal, but it sure beats letting destructive feelings accumulate. This strategy also helps to give you and your mate an edge in letting good feelings build up over time so that you'll reach the *Stability of Commitment* component of **LOVERS**. After all, isn't it your goal to enjoy a loving, stable marriage? Please don't allow your desire for vacation time with your husband to override your desire to remain **LOVERS** for life. The Second Wives Club is here to help you stay strong!

5. If your husband's children speak to you disrespectfully, a number of interwoven factors may be at work here. There's a fine line between a disrespectful child or teenager and one who feels enough at ease with an adult to speak without fear of being shushed. It is the adult's responsibility to teach

youngsters where the boundaries lie. An emotionally healthy child or teenager needs to have respect for the caretakers in her or his life in order to feel safe and secure. Furthermore, it is important to communicate your feelings to "his" children if you are addressed in a disrespectful manner. Speak softly but firmly as you let them know that both you and their father strongly disapprove of such behavior. Help them to understand that their disrespectful words may come from angry feelings on the inside. Perhaps they need assurance that you will encourage their father to always be close to them and that you are not a threat to them. Let them know that they are welcome in your home, and that your home is a "safe" place to talk about their feelings. If the children continue to speak to you disrespectfully, discuss it with your husband openly and privately. Subsequently, both of you should meet with the children and set down the rules and limitations. You must present a united, loving front to the children. The *Openness* and *Loyalty* components of LOVERS are vital to a relationship. As a second wife, you can see just how critical these points are to a healthy marriage. And you can also see how a child from your husband's previous marriage can present challenges, sometimes leading to much distress and tension.

6. How wonderful if you answered "true"! It is of major concern to a child of divorced parents that she/he still will remain a significant and special person in Dad's life. Some children fear that Dad's divorce from Mom is tantamount to Dad's

divorcing *them.* Where children and father had not shared a close relationship, you, as a second wife, could encourage a positive change. Cultivating and continuing the child–father bond has the added bonus of the children *not* being potential jack-in-the-boxes waiting to surprise you. Great going!

7. Children have a need to seek approval from their parents. In the case of a child of divorced parents, it is possible that carrying tales about Dad's new wife back to Mom at home is a means to this end. It is difficult to determine the motivation of a child who engages in this type of behavior. However, as adults, we can try to understand that these undesirable actions probably stem from insecurity and confusion on the part of a child—insecurity because of disruption to his/her family life, and confusion because of divided allegiance toward parents ("I love Daddy, but mostly Mommy takes care of me"). To help with these problems, assure the child that he/she is loved and is wanted in both mother's and father's homes despite the divorce. This consistent assurance will help stabilize the child and reduce the confusion about loyalty. Eventually, over time, the child will respond more positively when visiting and will not have the need to carry tales back from your house to Mom's.

8. It is seldom a good idea to have a child share a bed with parents. When this occurs, it is best to carry or walk the child back to her/his bed. Children's motives for wanting to share their parents' bed, with the exception of bad dreams, nightmares, or illness, usually stem from a need to feel secure, safe,

and loved. Depending on age and other factors, a child of divorced parents may have intense needs of that kind, which may present challenges. Alternatively, it is conceivable that the child's resentment toward you as a second wife is strong ("Only Mommy should be next to Daddy"). In both instances, patience and a continuing environment of love and safety are needed in order to help the child grow emotionally strong.

We hope that the insights gained from reading this checklist prove valuable in helping you uncover current and/or potential problems in your situation. The role of a second wife becomes complex when it is intertwined with the role of a stepmother. Unfortunately, "stepmothers" have acquired a negative and somewhat evil reputation. The minds of young children have been tainted with fairy tales that infuse stepmothers with despicable traits. No wonder these children of divorced parents approach their stepmothers with anxiety and trepidation! However, with patience, caring, and love, you can strive toward a healthier and happier relationship with your stepchildren ("his" children). The Second Wives Club has many members who are successful stepmothers.

The initial part of this chapter relates to young "first" children. But difficulties may occur in your marriage about the same time as your spouse's children have matured and are trying to find their way in the world. This can be very challenging for all concerned and sometimes sets the marital relationship on its ear. A perfect example of this complication is the case of Ned and Sandy, who were in their early fifties and had been married for over thirteen years. Sandy had been a successful interior designer, twice engaged but never married until Ned came along. Sandy was Ned's third wife; he claimed he was happy and content with Sandy until problems arose when his only child, Ellen, graduated from college. Ned was the sole owner of an important public-relations firm in a major city. He had built the business himself during his second marriage to Gloria. He and Gloria divorced after Ellen was born, and thereafter the child was raised by her mother. As more and more success came Ned's way, Ellen was given many material goods—"no" was not a word that she recognized. Much to Ned's dismay, his daughter was not given any responsibilities. She matured into a young woman concerned only with herself and feeling that the world owed her a living.

Ned enrolled his daughter in a prestigious small college where she was coddled into earning a bachelor's degree, with little effort on her part. This situation further perpetuated Ellen's myth of her sense of "entitlement."

Problems began to emerge soon after Ellen's graduation from college, when she became confused about her future. True to form, the young woman made meager efforts toward employment and soon asked her father for a job. Ned and Sandy discussed this turn of events with much anxiety, because it meant that Ellen would have to live with them.

Shortly after moving in with Ned and Sandy, Ellen's behavior and attitude became a major disruption in the home. She would borrow expensive clothes from Sandy without asking, steal money from Sandy's purse, and stay out all night. Sandy discovered that Ellen had been smoking pot in her room, and she disclosed this to Ned. Ned defended Ellen, claiming that she had had a difficult time adjusting to life after college. He felt that he and Sandy should not confront his daughter at this time. Sandy was angered at the decision Ned made; the couple argued bitterly. These arguments continued over a period of months, seriously damaging their relationship. Finally, when Sandy threatened to separate, Ned agreed to engage a professional counselor to help sort things out. Apparently, Ned was torn between his eagerness to help Ellen and his need to hold on to what had been a happy marriage.

When he met with me, Ned related the pertinent facts about his early marriages, about the emotional development of Ellen, and about his many wonderful years of marriage to Sandy. He said that he was very saddened that he hadn't been more instrumental in giving Ellen a sense of responsibility. He and Ellen's mother, Gloria, knew that this would be a problem in Ellen's adult years, but they weren't able to guide their daughter in this direction consistently. Ned, himself, bore an enormous feeling of responsibility toward his daughter and wanted to compensate for his early inadequate fathering by giving her a "good start" now.

DR. M.: Ned, your love for Ellen and concern for her is understandable. However, overcompensating now by making her life effortless seems to be a continuation of the indulgent style in which she was raised. This style might be labeled correctly as a sense of "entitlement." This happens sometimes when children are raised in an environment of excessive consumption without having to work for it. For example, if a baby is just learning to crawl and wants a ball from the other side of the room, what is his motivation to acquire the ball if his parents quickly give it to him? Why bother? This type of thinking seems to be the one in which Ellen was raised. Why perpetuate it?

NED: But Dr. Millian, Ellen's had a hard enough time. She's very bright, but she could hardly get through high school and college. (I was told she didn't make the effort.) Now that she's graduated from college, I want her to learn all about my business so one day she can be a partner. I've already started her off with a private office and a secretary. I want to give her incentive to work hard in the business.

DR. M.: Ned, try to relate the anecdote about the crawling baby to your daughter. Why should Ellen expend the effort to crawl (that is, learn your business) if you hand her the ball (that is, a private office with secretary) and spoon-feed her?

NED: So you're saying that I'm really not helping Ellen by giving her so much so soon. She has to learn to work hard to acquire skills needed in my business. I think I've equated good fathering with constant giving instead of cautious guiding.

———————

These insights constituted a major step for Ned, because he had had a distorted view of preparing his daughter for life. Now it was time to address Ellen's personal transgressions toward Sandy. Therefore, future sessions included Ned, Sandy, and Ellen. At the appropriate time, it was suggested that Ellen would benefit from individual counseling sessions.

A number of sessions were devoted to Ned and Sandy so that the concept of **LOVERS** could be introduced. It was important to the future of the couple's relationship that each component of the concept be evaluated, particularly those most relevant to them. What would your evaluation be of Ned and Sandy's LOVERS score? Scrutinizing this pair's dynamics will be of enormous help in determining *your* score.

It seemed that Ned and Sandy shared mutual *Respect* but failed to have the *Value of Trust* in one another's assessment of how to deal with Ellen's aberrant behavior. Their communication skills were not an issue; arguments did not curtail *Openness*. Further, the couple said that they had a deep, abiding love that seemed to grow with their years together. We then addressed *Loyalty,* which appeared to be one of the major conflicts within the marriage, resurfacing repeatedly. In other words, for whom should Ned have had greater loyalty—his wife or his daughter? Sandy expressed her sense of betrayal by Ned.

It followed that the *Stability of Commitment* component of LOVERS had been compromised due to the impact of inadequate *Value of Trust* and *Loyalty.* Once these issues were discussed thoroughly during our sessions, Ned and Sandy became aware of the need to address them to repair their marriage.

Sandy's jack-in-the-box was the result of her stepdaughter's sense of entitlement, which decreed that she didn't have to put forth effort to make gains. (This is such an unfair environment in which to raise a child!)

Ellen's anger and resentment toward Sandy was manifest in the young woman's abject disdain for Sandy's personal effects, and therefore Ellen caused a rift in Sandy and Ned's home. We are certain that you, as a second wife, can determine from this situation that it is imperative to dissolve challenges within your home. It doesn't matter if the challenge actually resides within your walls or someone else's;

the challenge is there and has to be confronted. Conflicts concerning children are sensitive and encapsulate a variety of emotions. Objectivity is what is required in order to attain resolution. If you and your spouse are unable to reach this goal, please do not hesitate to seek professional assistance.

The following story is an example of a child presenting a challenge that never actually enters the second wife's home. This particular circumstance may not be relevant to you because every scenario has distinct individuality. Nevertheless, in reviewing this story, it is certain that you will be able to gain valuable insights into your own dynamics and hopefully obtain more secrets of the Second Wives Club.

Richard, age thirty-two, had been married for three years to his childhood sweetheart, Victoria, when they decided to part amicably. Their daughter, Nicky, was two at the time of separation and three when the divorce took place. Richard shared custody of Nicky with Victoria, and both were loving and devoted parents. Richard spent much of his free time with his daughter, making her a very important part of his life.

Richard married Lisa when Nicky turned nine years of age. Richard and Lisa spent a lot of time to help Nicky feel as if she were an important member of their new family. Richard let his daughter know that they weren't a couple but a family of three. Nicky appeared to relish her new role as stepdaughter. Richard and Lisa insisted that Nicky accompany them on their honeymoon and selected a resort that catered to children.

It was during their honeymoon that Lisa first became aware that Nicky had changed from being the compliant, loving girl she and

Richard knew to being a real jack-in-the-box waiting to pop! They were stunned at the change in the child!

Nicky completely refused to participate in any of the activities offered by the resort for children. Furthermore, she demanded toys and gifts whenever the family was near a gift shop. Richard's refusal to acquiesce to Nicky's demands were met with temper tantrums worthy of a two-year-old, not a nine-year-old. When the tantrums didn't get Nicky what she wanted, she pouted and withdrew from conversations. In other words, Nicky regressed into very infantile behavior when she wasn't given her own way. No attempts at reasoning with her were successful.

Back at home, Richard and Lisa were discouraged but tried to analyze what had gone wrong with their best attempts at assuring Nicky of her place in their new family. A few weeks after their honeymoon, they invited Nicky to stay the weekend at their home. She refused, with no explanation. Repeatedly, Richard and Lisa asked Nicky to join them at their home. She turned down these requests every time. When Richard met with Nicky outside the home, he patiently asked his daughter to let him know the reasons for her behavior.

Finally, Richard and his ex-wife, Victoria, learned from Nicky that she didn't feel "special" anymore since Lisa had become her stepmother. She said that she had "bad" feelings about Lisa and that she knew the feelings were wrong to have. Nicky tearfully claimed that she felt she wasn't a nice person because of having these "bad" feelings.

At this point, Nicky's parents decided that professional intervention was needed. Family therapy was the modality selected in order to obviate the risk that the young girl would perceive herself as the "identified patient."

Over a period of time, Nicky's "bad" feelings about herself were discussed. A few sessions alone with the child were productive. In play therapy, the dynamics of Nicky's relationships with her father and Lisa were portrayed as she maneuvered dolls representing the three of them. It seemed that play therapy proved to be a safe environment in which Nicky could act out her emotions, rather than acting them out in destructive and regressive behavior in "real" life.

Nicky's fears about her place in her father's life were real, despite Richard's and Lisa's efforts to the contrary. In the girl's young eyes, her father was being taken from her by Lisa. The wedding had been a pivotal event that underscored Nicky's fears of being abandoned by Richard. The youngster's aberrant responses were the only ways she knew in which to communicate her feelings. In therapy, Nicky was taught to use words to express her feelings. If she was unable to find the words, she was encouraged to draw pictures to bring up her feelings. Eventually, Nicky adjusted to her father's remarriage and was able to see that nothing had changed between them. She was able to view Lisa in the role of loving stepmother rather than rival for her father's attention and love.

The role of second wife is rife with potential difficulties, and those in the form of an innocent but fearful child can be especially challenging. The child needs understanding, love, and a firm, guiding hand. In pursuit of this goal to integrate the child into *your* life with his father, however, you may come across many challenges. Overcoming these challenges can ensure your membership in the Second Wives Club. Good luck!

Challenge Number Three:
The Grandchildren
(THEY'RE REALLY SPECIAL—BUT AREN'T I ALSO?)

THIS CHAPTER ADDRESSES
issues surrounding your husband's grandchildren's impact on your
marriage. For some, this may not be an issue now or ever. Even if
this is the case, you may still want to read this chapter. It is helpful
to understand that over the years your husband has developed certain ways of relating to his children that have become ingrained.
Eventually, he probably will relate to his grandchildren in much the
same manner. This could be either positive or negative. If it's positive—wonderful! If it's negative, watch out! For example, if your husband overindulged his own children, there is a good chance that he
will go overboard with his grandchildren as well. Furthermore, if he
continues this extreme behavior toward his grandchildren, what
about *your* grandchildren? Will they receive the same treatment from

your husband when they are stepgrandchildren? What are your feelings about this? Your grandchild could become a jack-in-the-box waiting to surprise you!

Obviously, numerous factors determine whether a relationship between grandchildren and their grandparents is healthy or unhealthy. You must make an effort to uncover these factors in order to recognize and eliminate the unhealthy aspects of a relationship. The Second Wives Club will teach you effective responses to head off damage in your marriage.

Although the following story of Patrick and Chris may not seem relevant to you specifically, there is much to be learned from it regarding the power of grandchildren to create marital strife. The common denominator between this couple and you and your husband is the sensitive nature of the grandparent–grandchild bond and its potential to wreak havoc upon marriage. Challenges to marriages come in many forms—even grandchildren, love them as we do.

Patrick and Chris had been married for three years. Their case is indicative of the power of a grandfather's obsessive need for involvement in his grandson's life. This obsession nearly destroyed the marriage. Patrick, age sixty-three, had used his early years to build up his business, and in so doing, he acquired considerable wealth. His children were not a priority during this time; they had virtually "fatherless" childhoods. The children, now grown, were embittered and hostile toward Patrick. Because his children frequently reminded him of the emotional deprivation they had endured, Patrick vowed that he would spend a great deal of time with his two grandchildren. Only one grandchild, twelve-year-old Tommy, lived close by. Unconsciously, Patrick was trying to appease the anguish of his guilt, and at the same time, Tommy exploited his grandfather's vulnerability by manipulating him for attention and money. In time, this behavior planted seeds of discontent in the marriage; Chris was unhappy and called for intervention. Counseling was aimed toward helping Patrick recognize the dynamics of this unhealthy grandfather–grandson relationship, along with corrective methods to resolve the problems.

DR. M.: Chris and Patrick, you told me earlier in our session that you've been married for three years after knowing each other for a period of time. You seem to share many of the same values. You're both in your sixties and have been alone for a number of years. Now you've come together to enjoy your "golden years." You said that you married because of love, companionship, and the need to have someone "special" in your lives. Chris, you have spoken about problems that have arisen due to financial obligations on Patrick's part. However, this doesn't seem to be the issue that has brought you and Patrick here. Who would like to talk first?

CHRIS: Since it seems to be something that bothers me more than Patrick, why don't I start? I married Patrick because I love him dearly and want to spend a good portion of my days and nights with him. But that isn't happening. Patrick has an unusual relationship with his grandson, Tommy. The relationship goes way beyond a grandparent–grandchild relationship. Tommy has become very dependent on Patrick, but as though he were a pal his own age.

PATRICK: Chris, I have to interrupt. This is *your* opinion and not mine. Tommy and I have fun together and go many places he couldn't otherwise go.

DR. M.: Chris, why don't you give Patrick an example of what you're talking about, so that he can understand where you're coming from.

CHRIS: Dr. Millian, you have no idea how many times I've tried to give Pat examples of what's bothering me about this situation. His response is denial in the form of yelling at me in the most vile language I've ever heard. I can't have a conversation with him because of his screaming. He wasn't this way before we got married!

DR. M.: Patrick, it's clear that you feel very strongly about this bonding with your grandson. We'll get to that later. Please, Chris, give me an illustration of the problem as you see it.

CHRIS: A few months ago, we were invited to a surprise birthday party for one of our mutual friends. We both were looking forward to this special event, but three weeks before the party, Patrick said that he couldn't attend. The reason he gave was that Tommy's Boy Scout weekend campout was scheduled for the same night as our party. The scouts needed one more man to accompany the group or their campout would be canceled. Tommy's father could not go to his own son's outing, so Patrick was called into "service." I was to go to the party alone.

At this point in the conversation, Patrick exploded into a rage and screamed expletives at Chris for not understanding the "tight" spot in which he found himself. I intervened by telling him that such language was not OK in my office and that he would have his turn to speak.

Chris went on to give other examples of Patrick's putting Tommy's needs before hers and said that she felt betrayed and hurt by these insensitivities. She further said that she felt that Tommy was trying to sabotage their marriage by getting between them. Again, Patrick couldn't control his language and seemed unable to respond calmly and logically to Chris.

The issues here were, first, Patrick's way of responding impulsively and aggressively escalating the problems rather than rendering them manageable and open for discussion, and second, the very nature of the dispute, Patrick's need to be available constantly for Tommy. Additionally, it was puzzling to me why Chris was not a priority in Patrick's life. What were this grandfather's motivations in putting his grandson before his wife?

Patrick's reactions to Chris's complaints were filled with such anger that I felt joint marital counseling was unproductive at this juncture. The couple agreed that Patrick would begin individual counseling.

DR. M.: Patrick, during the joint session with Chris, it was quite apparent that she really struck a nerve in challenging your relationship with Tommy. It seems to be a very tender area for you. However, before we go into that, would you please talk to me about your relationship with your own children as they were growing up?

PATRICK: There was no relationship to speak of because I started my own business and wanted to make it "big" before I hit forty! The business was my child. I worked day and night. The kids and their mother had *everything*—a fabulous home, expensive toys, clothes, cars, and so forth. I thought *that* was being a great dad. Now the kids tell me differently. Now they say I was a rotten father. They say I was never there for them. They call me the "stranger." That really hurts!

DR. M.: Patrick, you did what you thought dads were supposed to do. In your generation, your way of relating to a child was through providing a home, food, and clothing. Dads of your era, as a rule, didn't do much more than that. Now we realize that a father is a vital and significant person in his child's emotional development. Although this insight is relatively new, it is an accepted part of our consciousness today. Your children were made aware of the need for their participation in their kids' lives. Yet because *your* generation's thinking is at odds with your *children's* thinking, you are being condemned as an inadequate father. Not so!

PATRICK: I never thought about it that way! Sure, I did the best I could with what I knew at the time. But since my kids told me that my best was not good enough, I felt terrible and guilty beyond imagination. I swore that I wouldn't be a "stranger" grandfather to my grandchildren. Being there for Tommy did help some of my guilt ease up. I couldn't make up for lost time with my own kids, but I wouldn't allow myself to repeat the mistakes of the past.

DR. M.: Can you see how some of your thinking of yourself as a negligent father influenced your attitude toward Tommy? You bought into your children's anger instead of helping them to understand that you showed them love the way you thought you were supposed to—through money. Their contemporary view of fatherhood seems to be a great improvement over your way, and you might let them know that. But also let them realize that you were influenced by your generation's thinking.

PATRICK: I can't wait to talk to them about this. I think I must have felt I was "losing" them and needed to connect with them through Tommy. (They've been rather withdrawn from me.) In the meantime, when Tommy yelled "jump" to me, I said, "How high?"

DR. M.: Sounds like Tommy might have taken advantage of his grandfather's need to be available to him, don't you think? Kids have a way of manipulating adults to their advantage when they know they can get away with it. Your grandchild is no different from other kids, so this is to be expected. But you don't have to go along with it.

PATRICK: Thanks for pointing that out to me. Looks like some changes will have to be made with my kids and with my grandchild. I can see that I've been going about things the wrong way.

DR. M.: I am also wondering, Patrick, whether your zeal to assuage your guilt overwhelmed your need to focus in on Chris and give your marriage the attention it deserves.

PATRICK: I knew all along that Chris had to be my first priority if our marriage was to work, but I was also so caught up in Tommy's life that I became lost. And then when she tried to talk to me about it, I couldn't handle being confronted with the truth. My tendency always was to yell first and think later.

DR. M.: That would seem to be your mode of operating in the past when confronted with a volatile situation. There are better ways to handle problems than to respond impulsively. At our next session, let's talk about some behavioral techniques that will help you control your impulsiveness. It must make you feel awful to be out of control, and it could be intimidating for Chris.

It was helpful for Patrick to become aware of the nuances of his relationship with his own children and how these impacted on him and Tommy. He then was able to put these relationships into perspective and forever close the jack-in-the-box—no more surprises! Patrick's explosive verbal responses to Chris and his simultaneous impulsiveness were addressed by simple behavioral exercises (see chapter 11). Patrick's underlying need to respond so destructively was lessened by understanding the reasons behind it—basically, guilt and avoidance of reality.

On examining the case of Chris and Patrick, we can see that divorced men frequently are penalized twice. They might be emotionally and logistically separated not only from their children but from their grandchildren as well. It is no mystery or surprise that children internalize their parents' habits, idiosyncrasies, and attitudes. Some adult children are angry because of their parents' divorce. Accordingly, grandparents may be punished unfairly by their grandchildren because the youngsters are too immature to understand the facets and the dynamics of divorce. Consequently, they may adopt their parents' attitudes toward divorce and in the process create antagonism toward their grandfathers. This, then, becomes a powerful intrusion in the guise of an "innocent" child.

The LOVERS concept was used in joint sessions to redirect Chris and Patrick. As you evaluate this couple in light of LOVERS, which do you perceive as their only intact component? This story illustrates a problem particular to Chris and Patrick, but the ideas in it are universal and applicable in some part to many. It would be helpful to discover the parts of this story most relevant for you!

The constituent of LOVERS found to be strongest in the relationship of Chris and Patrick was *Love*. There was no doubt that each partner loved the other. There was also no doubt that this love was being challenged and sabotaged. Therefore, every other component of LOVERS was affected adversely. It looked like Chris needed the help of the Second Wives Club!

Here's a quiz you can take to help you explore and examine the possible challenges your husband's grandchildren may present. The quiz will stimulate your awareness of an unhealthy "grand" relationship. Once these challenges are identified, please try one or more of the suggestions in the checklist. These suggestions can be pivotal in your movement toward enhancing your marriage.

Q U I Z

Mark T *for "true" and* F *for "false."*
Honesty is always the best you-know-what!

_____ 1. My husband's trips to visit his grandchild(ren) require absences from home for lengthy periods of time.

_____ 2. My husband prefers to baby-sit less frequently than I.

_____ 3. I disagree with my husband that grandchildren should have free reign in our home (for example, eat in the living room or den, not put away their belongings, and so on).

_____ 4. Discipline is only the parents' job, never the grandparents', according to my husband.

_____ 5. My husband's grandchildren live in a foreign country. He insists that our vacations be spent visiting them.

_____ 6. We sometimes have to go to extraordinary lengths to alternate seeing our respective grandchildren, to keep things "fair."

_____ 7. My husband's teenage grandchildren will not attend family functions if I am invited along with their grandmother (his former wife).

_____ 8. I realize that we all are biased toward our own grandchildren, but my spouse consistently defers to his grandkids at *my* grandkids' expense.

C H E C K L I S T

1. If you answered "true" to this statement, your mate's jaunts to visit his grandchild probably are disturbing to you. The geographic location of grandchildren can be upsetting, because distance leads to prolonged absences. Of course, as a second wife sensitive to the needs of her spouse, you can't fault him for wanting contact with his grandchildren. On the other hand, if that contact jeopardizes your marriage, the "fault" is irrelevant. Your marital happiness is what counts! How can you give him the message that "I married you to have a companion, but your grandchildren are taking up too much of your time"? It is apparent that such a response will result in ill feelings between the two of you. Far better to say, "I married you because I love you and want to enjoy your wonderful company. I understand how much your grandchildren mean to you. Let's visit them together or have them visit with us here at home." In this way, you've confronted the challenge of his grandchildren by eliminating the stress of the problem and simultaneously solidified the bond with your husband. Get rid of those wispy bits of your husband's past lurking

in the shadows and encourage joint visits with his grand-children—and with yours.

2. Most women mark this statement "true," so it comes as no surprise. Generally speaking, females are more amenable to the nitty-gritty of baby-sitting than males. There always are exceptions, but usually it's the guys who balk at being respon-sible for grandchildren in the absence of their parents. Differences in opinions and preferences are an acceptable and inevitable part of a relationship. It is how a couple goes about exercising those opinions that is significant. This is where the *Openness* component of **LOVERS** comes in. The communication skills of partners are vital at all times but par-ticularly when basic philosophies of family relationships are polarized. In other words, when you as second wife want to baby-sit once a week and your spouse insists that once a month is sufficient, you two are on opposite sides. Compromise and understanding are the key to resolution here. One might suggest baby-sitting twice a month as an acceptable compro-mise. The compromise also might reflect the number of grandchildren you have between the two of you, how much free time you have, the state of your health, and your chil-dren's needs. See chapter 11 for strategies on problem-solving through better communication skills. Improving these skills is particularly important if conflicts arise between baby-sitting your spouse's grandchildren and yours—and whose grand-kids take priority. Keeping a careful calendar of your child-care schedules can help you plan ahead and alternate

baby-sitting with respective grandchildren. Both honing up your communication skills and planning ahead can prevent surprises from bursting out of the jack-in-the-box!

3. Should you and your spouse be in agreement on rules for the grandchildren, there is no problem. But however trivial this may sound, one's notions on raising children could be a point of contention in a marriage. This holds for grandchildren as well, despite recognition that the parents ultimately determine the values in which a child is raised. It is obvious that when *your* grandchildren come to visit, you feel more comfortable in restricting them to the kitchen while eating than you do "his" grandkids. They're *your* grandkids, and it's OK. Far more delicate a situation occurs when your spouse's grandchildren are involved. You certainly don't want to chance them pulling rank on you: "He's my grandpa and I'll listen to him, not you." This scenario becomes especially touchy when your husband's views of children are far more liberal than yours: "Kids should feel free to go where they please in a home. I wasn't when I was a kid, and it really bothered me." If you responded "true" to this statement, it is best to be open but firm with your spouse on this point. Communicating your values to one another leads to getting an A+ on the *Openness* component of LOVERS. Additionally, being sensitive to each other's values of what is important in one's home underscores the *Loyalty, Respect,* and *Empathy* components of LOVERS. Your goal is a satisfying and harmonious marriage for life. Good going!

4. Discipline of grandchildren can become a contentious issue because grandparents often feel conflicted in this area. A response of "true" to this statement might indicate that your spouse has a strong need to "engage" his grandchildren at all costs. Emotions involved in the grandparent–grandchild relationship may be an extension of feelings such as guilt, fear, jealousy, and so on. Your husband might harbor some of these emotions unconsciously as a result of his divorce. If so, his efforts to reduce the anxiety may result in his hesitation to set limits on the grandkids. These feelings, compounded by the special love we have for grandchildren, can result in an extremely intense and volatile drama. There are many fine books available on the importance of imposing discipline and structure on children. Being grandparents doesn't obviate this need. The grandparent's "right" to "spoil" grandchildren has no bearing on inadequate enforcement of basic discipline and good manners when you're with them. It's best to discuss these issues with your husband as well as with his children. It helps tremendously if you stay focused on remaining LOVERS for life.

5. Here you are, free and clear from work and other responsibilities. You've either cut back or retired. It's time to travel and time to enjoy each other. However, it seems that your interpretation of "enjoy each other" is at odds with your spouse's. According to your mate, every vacation must center around visiting "his" grandchildren because of the vast distance involved. "Not so," say you. "I love grandchildren, too,

but I want to see the world with you." Compromise and communication are key issues to your salvation here. In other words, be open with your husband. Be loving and be firm. Try to understand that your husband may feel guilty that his divorce might have adversely affected his children and grandchildren. Therefore, the geographic distance that precludes easy get-togethers may be a factor in exacerbating his guilt. Alternating vacations or meeting the grandchildren halfway may be options. The point is to consider other avenues of visitation. Remember, you became your husband's second wife because you love him; this implies loyalty and respect. Don't let "his" grandchildren become overwhelming challenges in your marriage. A stable marriage is one in which both individuals are sensitive and loyal to the needs of the other.

6. The bottom line here is that you and your spouse are willing to go to extremes to keep things "fair." Although it is accepted that "life is not fair," the fact that two partners work toward making that phrase moot is to their credit. You both are to be complimented if you answered "true" to this statement. You are officially a successful practicing member of the Second Wives Club!

7. Family functions are an area where one must tread lightly. It could put a strain on the event if your husband's former wife ("their" grandmother) and you are in joint attendance. Your best intentions may be to put hostility aside for the sake of the children and grandchildren. Even when the best intentions

prevail, watch out—turmoil straight ahead! It is conceivable that your husband's teenage grandkids want to avoid any kind of scene. Another possibility is that "his" grandchildren are angry with you and their grandfather and want to hurt you by their rebuff. The scenarios are infinite, as are the reasons for your being excluded. As the second wife, you definitely have obstacles to overcome. It would be far better for you to concentrate on your goals in life—that of a fruitful marriage— rather than declaring World War III over the slight. Being LOVERS for life, not a sparring partner, is your objective!

8. If you responded "true," you might consider the following: it is human nature to be especially sensitive to the needs of one's own family. However, it is possible that your husband is not aware of the extremes to which he takes this bias. One's loyalties sometimes can become challenged when confronted with grandchildren. Perhaps your spouse feels that *you* will be attentive and supportive of *your* grandchildren; consequently, he must do the same for his. Speak to your husband about having an even hand with both sets of grandchildren and being in the "same corner." Why assume an adversarial role with your mate? It is critical for you both to be loyal to each other, support each other emotionally, and be mutually sensitive to each other's needs. Here, too, communication as a means of getting through an uncomfortable situation is the key. Grandchildren should not cause a rift in your marriage. Practice the secrets of the Second Wives Club, and soon you will be LOVERS for life despite any challenges that may arise.

Another scenario pertaining to grandchildren that may surprise you is exemplified in the case of Tony and Maryann, a couple in their mid-fifties who had been married for over ten years. Only Maryann had a grandchild. The couple's marriage had been fraught with conflict from the beginning, primarily due to Tony's demands for exclusive attention. Therefore, in the first few years, Maryann indulged her spouse enthusiastically. The problems came to a head soon after the much-heralded arrival of Maryann's granddaughter, Marie.

In our initial meeting, I asked each of them to tell me their point of view on what brought them to counseling, so I could understand what was going on. I had scarcely got my words out when a very agitated Maryann interrupted.

MARYANN: Dr. M., I love Tony a lot, and for years and years I tried to make him happy. This meant that I couldn't see my daughter or my friends—except with him. I worked, came home, cooked, cleaned, and spent evenings watching television with Tony.

TONY: That's what wives do! You married me. We spend time together. That's why I got married. Why do you need anyone else?

MARYANN: We used to fight over this issue plenty, and I'd wind up giving in to him because he wore me down.

DR. M.: Maryann, what's different about the present time? You went along with Tony all those years. What's changed?

TONY: That's what I'd like to know. I liked things as they were, not now!

MARYANN: I've waited a long, long time for a grandchild.

TONY: So have I. I'm still waiting.

MARYANN: I want to be with Marie and watch her growing up. I want to take her places, have fun with her. I know that some of that time takes me away from Tony. I told you before, Tony, that you've held me back from seeing my family and friends, and I didn't like it one bit. I gave in to you to keep you quiet because I didn't want trouble and didn't want you to question my love for you. It was easier that way but I see it was the wrong way.

TONY: Dr. Millian, please tell my wife that married people are together all the time. They don't go out separately; they're always together. If they don't want to be with each other, why get married? Doesn't make sense. Maybe Maryann doesn't really love me. . . .

DR. M.: Tony, people get married for a whole variety of reasons, the most important of which is the love they feel for one another. You seem to be saying that the quality of love in a marriage is determined by the couple wanting to be in each other's company constantly. People need time away from their mates also—breathing time, as it were. This has nothing to do with love, but it has everything to do with the health of a marriage. It seems that you're trying to put severe restrictions on Maryann to ensure her love for you. Don't you think that your approach is having the opposite effect on your wife?

TONY: All I hear about from Maryann is her little Marie. Ever since Marie was born, Maryann and I are together less and less. I feel like an afterthought—not important to her.

MARYANN: Tony, I ask you along all the time. Why can't you think of Marie as *your* granddaughter, too? She always asks for "Papa"!

TONY: She's not really my granddaughter. I have no grandchild, and I won't *ever* have one because my son and his wife can't have kids of their own!

At this point tears came to Tony's eyes. We had three issues here: first, Tony's confusion between love/marriage and exclusivity of time; second, Tony's pain at not having his own grandchild; and third, Maryann's prior timidity on asserting her right to have time separate from Tony.

Therapy addressed each item, one by one. Tony came to be receptive to the idea regarding the need for couples to enjoy separate areas of their lives. He was helped to understand that a smothering love is not one that grows. Individual counseling with each person addressed the key underlying factors. Tony's hurt had the double impact of agonizing over both his son's despair of being childless and his own pain of not having a grandchild. Maryann had said that she felt very disloyal to Tony when she desired time away from him. In time she was helped to understand that she had a perfect right to see friends and family separately from Tony. She was given training in assertiveness and encouraged to feel that she could be more open with Tony.

We discussed the *Loyalty* component of LOVERS at their next joint session. I emphasized that, along with loyalty, the other parts of LOVERS that were affected as a result of their problem were *Openness*, *Stability*, and *Empathy*. We worked through some problem-solving techniques (see "Communication Skills" in chapter 11), utilizing role-playing as a means of building up skills in this area.

After reviewing this Second Wives Club member's story, you can see that the influence of grandchildren need not necessarily be that of your spouse's grandchildren. In the case of Maryann and Tony, the challenge emerged due to the *absence* of a spouse's grandchild!

Be aware that you as a second wife face many potential challenges. Each challenge has the potential to cause a rift in a wonderful relationship with your husband. Discovering your challenges early and taking positive steps to eliminate them can point you and your mate in the right direction. Try to keep the specialness of grandchildren just that—special and precious. Using the insights and the skills you've learned in this chapter, you can create happy times!

Challenge Number Four:
The Mother-in-Law

(DO THEY DESERVE THEIR BAD REP—OR WHAT?)

WE ARE ALL FAMILIAR WITH the persona of the stereotypical mother-in-law—a woman bedeviled with an intrusive and critical nature. Mothers-in-law are derided in comedy sketches, in soap operas, in books, and in real life. Do all mothers-in-law live up to their nefarious reputation? Obviously not. But enough of them seem to play so powerful a role in the dynamics of their son's marriage as to warrant mention in this book. Many may have had misgivings about their son's divorce and remarriage. Their reservations may manifest as anger, bitterness, and outrage toward the second wife.

Let's examine the case of Margot and Lonny in order to understand the impact of a mother-in-law on a second marriage. Lonny's mother, Diane, had always wanted a daughter. Lonny, her only child, was a boy in every sense of the word—strong, aggressive, and possessing a predilection toward sports and, later on, women. Lonny first married at age twenty-one to Meredith, his high school sweetheart. Meredith was sweet, naïve, compliant, and eager to please. Not having a close relationship with her own mother propelled Meredith into a bond with Diane, who soon took the role of the nurturing, wise, all-giving mother. Meredith trusted Diane with every aspect of her life, relying on her judgment to make even the most minute decisions. Diane reveled in this situation and used it as a tool to gain a permanent foothold in her son's life. In essence, Diane finally had a "daughter." Over time, Diane became overtly critical of Meredith's mother. The criticism drove a wedge further between mother and daughter, thus ensuring Diane of her place in Meredith's life.

Meredith and Lonny presented Diane with a granddaughter after the first year of marriage. Diane's happiness in having a "daughter" and granddaughter was immeasurable. All was going well in her life. In contrast, son Lonny was in despair over his marriage and asked for a divorce. Diane pleaded with Lonny to reconsider, even threatening him by cutting him out of her very considerable will. Lonny was determined. After the divorce, Meredith and the baby relocated to reside with her parents, some three thousand miles away from Diane and Lonny. Diane alternated between being desolate and outraged at her son's "selfish" decision to divorce.

Diane was distant from her son after the divorce. Lonny was hurt and confused at his mother's behavior; the divorce had been difficult for him. To compound the trauma, Lonny assumed responsibility for his mother's loneliness and unhappiness due to the loss of her granddaughter and "daughter."

This, then, was the environment within which Margot and Lonny became husband and wife, two years after Lonny's divorce. Their love was strong; they knew what they wanted, and what they wanted was each other—but how high a price were they willing to pay? Diane seemed to welcome her new daughter-in-law into her family with an open heart and an open mind. Her behavior indicated that here again she recognized an opportunity to create a daughter from her son's wife. At Lonny's insistence, he and Margot found an apartment that was only two blocks away from Diane. In turn, the mother delighted in the close proximity and made Sunday dinner a ritual at her home. Additionally, Diane was generous with the young couple and gifted them with a household of furnishings—but insisted on joining their shopping excursions. Diane offered her love and generosity to Margot and Lonny—but at an enormous price.

Six months into the marriage, the couple was torn apart with arguments stemming from the prehensile hold that Diane had over Lonny and her attempts to twist Margot into what she wanted her to become—a dutiful, faithful, compliant "daughter." Margot, however, would have none of that. She was grateful that Diane accepted her into the family and tried to respond to her as a loving daughter-in-law. But Margot soon discovered that Diane wanted much more than what she, as a young wife, was willing to give to anyone—her whole, entire self. Diane once more wanted her own version of what she perceived and needed a "daughter" to be.

Lonny, out of guilt, stood by his mother and tried to persuade his wife to be more empathic to Diane. He urged Margot to be the loving, submissive daughter. After all, Lonny argued, his mother meant well, and her demands emanated from love.

Lonny and Margot were helped in counseling to understand about a family's need to determine and adhere to "boundaries." In other words, it is important to clarify where each family member's needs and responsibilities begin and end. Specifically, in Lonny's case, the boundaries were merged in both mother's and son's minds. But Diane's goal in life should have been to find fulfillment for herself in emotionally mature ways, rather than through another person. Her almost obsessive need to have a daughter was an issue to be explored in counseling. It was important for Lonny to understand his mother's need and its impact on him and on the marriage.

Lonny's part in boundary confusion lay buried in the muck of guilt he felt regarding his mother. In his mind, he had inflicted pain and suffering on Diane after divorcing his first wife. His mother felt abandoned by her quasi "daughter" and felt further devastated by the "loss" of her granddaughter. Lonny's deep sense of responsibility toward his mother riveted him to live close to her and to allow her to control him via his wife. The many efforts to please Diane were Lonny's attempts to assuage his guilt. In therapy, Lonny was helped to understand the conflicts emanating from his confusion (merging) of family boundaries. Discussions ensued regarding his needs versus the needs of himself and his wife. Lonny's responsibilities toward Diane were examined and clarified in the context of an adult son. There was no question of Lonny's love and respect for his wife; however, loyalty remained a key issue throughout the sessions. In other words, to which woman—mother or wife—should Lonny be more loyal? The young man was emphatic in declaring his loyalty to Margot. However, he agonized that he couldn't bear to sacrifice his degree of loyalty to Diane in order to uphold his loyalty to Margot.

All of these factors were central to the marital conflict between Lonny and Margot. Therapy helped Lonny to work through these issues and to understand that his obligations to himself, his wife, and their marriage were critical to the success of the relationship. Further, he was helped to understand that upholding his loyalty to Margot did not necessarily require that he compromise his loyalty to his mother. These two loyalties were separate entities within separate boundaries. Once Lonny assimilated these new insights, he was able to get past the guilt he had felt in causing his mother unhappiness over his past and present relationships. Lonny was able to let go of these unconscious feelings when he realized that his mother was responsible for her own happiness and that it was not her son's obligation to provide it for her.

On the other hand, Margot was urged to be more sensitive to her mother-in-law's distress and loss. She was reminded that partners in a relationship should strive toward being LOVERS. Margot was helped to understand that the component of *Empathy* in LOVERS was just as critical to a successful marriage as the component of *Loyalty*.

This Second Wives Club story is just one example of a rather typical conflict involving a mother-in-law, that is, the question of loyalties. Lack of empathy, guilt, and confusion of loyalties can wreak havoc on an otherwise amicable marital relationship. Although it may not be the "fault" of the second wife, such conflicts certainly can render her a prime candidate for help from the Second Wives Club.

The following questions will help you to assess whether or not your mother-in-law has become a serious concern in your relationship with your husband.

Mark T *for "true" and* F *for "false."*

_____ 1. My mother-in-law constantly visits unannounced.

_____ 2. My husband refuses to listen to me when I have a problem with his mother.

_____ 3. My mother-in-law insists on knowing what I pay for things—down to the dishtowels.

_____ 4. My mother-in-law immediately asks for my husband when I answer the phone.

_____ 5. My mother-in-law probes our children with personal questions about me.

_____ 6. My mother-in-law is a loving presence in my life.

_____ 7. My husband has become his mother's maintenance/repairman for her home.

_____ 8. My mother-in-law tells other family members about problems we discuss.

C H E C K L I S T

1. If your mother-in-law visits unannounced, it could be indicative that your mother-in-law has a problem with boundaries. In other words, her need to pop into your home whenever she chooses is primary in her mind. It may not occur to her that you and your family have other needs and certainly a right to

privacy. It would seem that her boundaries merge into yours. Separation from her son, and realization that he has his own priorities as an adult may be at issue here. You and your husband need to establish a set of guidelines for visits. On one hand, you don't want to offend her; on the other hand, friendly specified visits or phone calls should be encouraged.

2. Yes, it is a great benefit to your marriage if your husband has an open mind when problems relate to his mother. However, when you involve your husband to the extent that a two-person problem escalates into a three-person problem, a triangle is formed. And this triangle can lead to big trouble! It is far better to restrict any conflicts between two individuals to the individuals themselves and *not* broaden the base of the difficulty. After all, why make a skirmish into World War III? In other words, discuss the problem directly with your husband's mother before involving him.

3. Answering "true" may indicate one or both of the following problems: Just because a person "insists" on knowing something does not mean that you have to comply with their demands. Please ask yourself why you are not able to say "no" to your mother-in-law. Do you have this difficulty only with her or with others in your life as well? If the latter is true, it may indicate that your need to please others—and thus win their approval—outweighs your need to please yourself. Why not practice *enlightened selfishness?* This term does not encourage you to be selfish in the greedy, self-absorbed sense of the word, but it does urge you to take good care of

yourself and your needs. To illustrate, a hungry waitress cannot do her best work if her own stomach is grumbling. She has to be satiated, that is, she must take care of her own needs prior to helping others. Another possibility for your problem with your mother-in-law's inquisitiveness simply may be that she has a need to be intrusive and controlling for reasons particular to her. The satisfaction of her need, however, is *not* your problem. Take it from the Second Wives Club: There is no sense letting *her* problem be the catalyst for rifts in your marriage!

4. If you answered "true," change things around a bit the next time she calls. You might say, "I'll put Tom on in a minute. I was looking forward to having a chat with you first." If that doesn't work after a few tries, you might take her out to lunch and ask her why she insists on speaking only to your husband. If there is a problem, usually it is far better to find out in the beginning rather than let it get out of hand. Sometimes there's a simple answer that portends a simple solution.

5. This situation is touched on in another chapter, but it bears repeating here. Some people feel that they can use children to their advantage in order to glean personal information about adults in their household. It's unfair. It's unnecessary. But it's common practice. It is always best not to put children in such a compromising situation. No child should be put in such a position. Therefore, the best approach, again, is the direct approach—talk to your mother-in-law. Speaking with her on a one-to-one basis does not necessarily mean a

confrontation. Use diplomacy. Explain that her inquiry of the children into private family matters has made them uncomfortable. Suggest that in the interests of continuing to be the loving mother-in-law/grandmother, it would be best to circumvent the kids and speak to you instead. This is a delicate situation, and you have to keep your head about you.

6. To answer this affirmatively, you have to be one of the luckiest women alive! How wonderful to feel so highly about your husband's mother! This kind of relationship is a sparkling and wonderful asset to your marriage as well as a tribute to you and to her.

7. If your husband is his mother's maintenance/repairman, this can be a test of your patience with the mother–son relationship. Such a situation is common not only to second wives but to first wives as well. If your husband's role before marriage has been to be his parents' "keeper of the home," it seems that the job continues and continues. This is exacerbated when the parents are elderly or when the mother lives alone. Of course, in good conscience, you would not want your husband to withhold his help from his mother. After all, you married him partially because he is a giving and loving man. But conflicted feelings emerge when his mother's demands on his free time become excessive to the point of sacrificing your family's needs. In order to prevent ill feelings and resentment between all parties concerned, it would be advantageous to work out a schedule of necessary chores agreed upon by everyone and, barring emergencies, to uphold it.

The Second Wives Club shows you ways that this situation can be worked out satisfactorily for all!

8. If your mother-in-law tells others about the problems that you discuss, this unfortunate situation can be precipitous to a strained relationship between mother-in-law and daughter-in-law. A reserved attitude toward your mother-in-law can be unpleasant for you and can impact your marriage negatively. If your dealings with your husband's mother generally are positive to the point where you really desire a sincere and loving relationship, why not openly discuss your concerns with her? Always state your case in positive terms, such as, "I'm really eager to have a great relationship with you and have you be a meaningful part of our lives. However, it is important to me that our private discussions remain just that—private." Approaching your husband's mother in that light should ensure a successful membership in the Second Wives Club.

Needless to say, some of the comments above may be relevant to fathers-in-law as well as mothers-in-law. Traditionally, however, it appears to be the mother-in-law with whom these issues emerge. In order to sustain the key elements of a wonderful marriage, establishing and maintaining a good relationship with in-laws is well worth your efforts.

Please keep reminding yourself that your ultimate goal with your husband is to remain **LOVERS** for life. Getting past any problems with your mother-in-law is an essential part of achieving this wonderful goal of lifelong love.

Challenge Number Five: The Friends

(THEIR FRIENDS, OUR FRIENDS—
ARE THEY REALLY FRIENDS?)

THIS CHAPTER ADDRESSES
some of the possibly damaging contributions of "old" friendships from a prior marriage. The divided loyalty of these friends may compromise the unity and strength of a new marriage. As the second wife, you have probably experienced the conflict regarding "their" friends. You might ask yourself, "Am I merely being tolerated because I am his new wife?" And you might be uncomfortable in the company of "their" friends. Trust and loyalty, the basic necessities in a friendship, may be hard-won in the relationship that you have with their friends. You might wonder if they would carry tales back to your husband's former wife. Or you might question if they now are committed entirely to you and have become "your" friends.

Another possibility is that the divided loyalty of friends may relate specifically to your husband. For example, perhaps their friends chose to maintain the friendship with only your husband's ex-wife. Rejection elicits hurt and angry feelings. If your husband is predisposed toward low self-esteem, such feelings may be rekindled. He might wonder why friends aligned with her and not him. The rejections might serve to validate any guilt your husband's friends may have regarding his divorce. This sequence of events—friends' rejections, husband's emotional response—may negatively impact your marriage and lead to a serious rift. The influence of prior friends has the capacity to tear asunder a marriage.

The following story depicting issues of loyalty and perceived betrayal by friends will demonstrate the dilemma in which one Second Wives Club member found herself.

Rob and his friend from college, Steve, had been inseparable and continued to be close when their respective wives, Sheila and Ann, also became friends. Rob had been unhappy for most of the eight years of his marriage. For one thing, Sheila had decided that she really did not want to have children, contrary to her prenuptial discussion with Rob. This situation constituted a major disappointment in Rob's life, which led to continuous arguments. Despite Rob's expressed dissatisfaction with their marriage, Sheila refused to seek counseling. Their marital relationship steadily deteriorated, and eventually, Rob no longer felt love for Sheila. Following a particularly vitriolic argument, Rob used the confrontation as an excuse to leave home. Subsequently, he asked for a divorce, and in so doing, he evoked fierce responses of both refusal and rage from Sheila. Sheila was hurt and demeaned, the personification of a woman scorned.

Shortly thereafter, Sheila advised friends Ann and Steve of Rob's decision to leave. Hearing only Sheila's side of the story, the distraught friends angrily turned against Rob. Steve, in effect, denied Rob the comfort and understanding of a dear friend in time of need. As the months went by, their friends acted as spies for Sheila, becoming her allies and reporting Rob's social activities to her. Rob felt greatly betrayed by Steve. Rob's feelings of unworthiness were compounded by the guilt that inevitably resulted from his leaving Sheila. He started to doubt himself and to deny the reality of the poor quality of his marriage. He asked himself, "So what if I was unhappy? What kind of person can I be to hurt another so much?"

Rob married Irene two years after the divorce and sought the blessing of his friend Steve. His attempts to renew their friendship were thwarted and completely unacknowledged. Rob became withdrawn and depressed, leaving Irene confused and helpless in the matter. Not wanting to inflict his emotional despair upon Irene, Rob distanced himself from her. Irene interpreted her husband's withdrawal as rejection. These feelings then escalated into a strained relationship between the couple. Slowly, they started drifting away from each other. It was apparent that the influence of former friends had triggered dissension in this otherwise loving marriage. Irene and Rob knew that their relationship was in trouble and that intervention was imperative for its survival.

DR. M.: From what you both have told me during our initial interview, your marriage has gone well insofar as you love and trust one another, and you *want* your relationship to work. You each are very willing to put in whatever effort it takes to get past the hurdles that you're encountering. Those hurdles seem to be in the form of early friendships interfering in your lives. Before we get to that, can you give me a little background on yourselves, such as your families, Rob's prior marriage, and whatever ever else you care to talk about?

IRENE: I come from a working-class family where both parents worked hard and long hours just to feed my brother and me. Dad worked as an engineer for Conrail and Mom ran a doctor's office. My childhood was what I'd call normal and uneventful. My parents were always there for us, and we felt pretty good about ourselves. My early relationships with guys were good ones, but I didn't want to settle for just anyone. Then Rob came along, and he was what I wanted. I'm glad I waited!

DR. M.: Thanks, Irene. We can fill in the blanks later on, as needed. Rob, what about you?

ROB: My folks were all involved in my mother's brother's business, which was a small landscaping company. I was the only child—Mom almost died when she had me—and I felt very wanted by my parents. They did whatever they could for me. Problems came up in school that gave me a lot of heartache. It's hard to talk about.

DR. M.: Sometimes it's very painful to recall our early childhood, Rob. Please remember that you are today a composite of all the experiences you've gone through in the past. Your experiences, together with a constantly spiraling interaction with your temperament, led to the development of your personality—who you are right now. In order to help you, I need to understand what made you into the person you are today. If you feel that this is too hurtful at this moment, we can discuss it another time—or alone.

ROB: No, no. Irene knows the whole story and I want to be open with you so you can really help us. You see, when I was a boy, I was greatly overweight—so much so that the kids in school used to make fun of me, tease me, taunt me, poke at me. I'd go home crying, not wanting to go back. I didn't have one friend. Nobody wanted to speak to me. This went on throughout junior high school—I really got fat when I became eleven years old—and it followed me into high school. I grew up in a small community, and the same kids were together the entire period of time in school.

DR. M.: What did your parents do about it?

ROB: We couldn't move, so we couldn't change schools. They went down to the teachers and the principal. No one was able to help. I suffered the whole time and had no friend but the refrigerator. It was lonely.

DR. M.: I can only imagine the agony you went through as a child. The telling of this very traumatic childhood is difficult for you.

ROB: After high school, I went to a two-year college away from home and was able to start making a life for myself. I took control of my weight with the help of the first real friend that I ever made— Steve. It seemed that my past didn't follow me to school, and I was able to start all over. Thanks to Steve—and soon other friends— I learned how to make friends and keep friends.

DR. M.: Now I can understand why your friendship with Steve means so much to you. He was instrumental in your early years as a young man. He helped you to battle the hurts that were inside of you. He helped you feel that you had value.

ROB: Yes. Steve meant a lot to me. So when we got out of college and married, you can imagine how thrilled Steve and I were when our wives became friends. It meant so much to both of us! We saw each other two or three times a week because we lived only ten miles apart. At first, I thought I had everything—a wife who I thought loved me, a good job, healthy parents, and my best friend close by! Little did I know!

Rob then unfolded the story of his marriage with Sheila and how their relationship deteriorated, beginning the second year. The most significant factor in this deterioration centered on the issue of children. Rob and she were at opposite ends: Rob wanted to start a family; Sheila was adamant in her refusal, and without Rob's knowledge, she had her tubes tied to prevent pregnancy. At this point Rob moved out of their home, saying that there was no reasoning with Sheila and that he couldn't live in such turmoil.

Counseling consisted of a dual approach: remedial measures addressing short- and long-term problems both within Rob and within his marriage to Irene.

It was clear to me as a therapist that Rob's unconscious need for love and approval at all costs were of long duration, and stemmed from the patterns of early childhood rejection by peers. Helping Rob to become aware of the power of his needs and how to work through them became long-term goals in our sessions. Helping Irene to understand Rob's needs in order to enhance her empathy skills became an important goal as well.

Short-term goals were needed to give Rob the behavioral tools necessary to resolve the immediate problems. For example, methods such as thought stopping (inserting a pleasant thought into his mind to substitute for a negative one), visualization techniques, and the

Progressive Muscle Relaxation Exercises (see chapter 11) were taught to Rob. These techniques provided him with almost immediate relief from the damaging effects of his near-constant use of negative self-statements. Rob's perception of himself was a reflection of the cruel ways in which his peers had treated him.

As Rob progressed in therapy, we were able to integrate his new awareness and strength into his marriage. The couple's insights relevant to themselves expanded, and they were able to establish a firm foundation in their relationship. I introduced them to the LOVERS concept of a healthy, glowing marriage. They readily understood which parts of LOVERS were absent from their union. In particular, the *Empathy* component was crucial to the couple's progress in counseling. As you look at the scenario of Rob and Irene, what is *your* take on the missing components? And how do these inadequacies relate to your situation? Remember, each couple's dynamics differ, but they all center around the importance of factors in the LOVERS concept. Every second wife can reap benefits from learning about others' ratings in the LOVERS evaluation. A friend can be a joy forever—or a potential jack-in-the-box waiting to pop!

The preceding story has acquainted you with one aspect of challenges from friends—that of ambiguous loyalty. Other variations on friendship themes are equally destructive. Some of these variations will be explored by way of case examples later in this chapter.

As seen in the case of Irene and Rob, one of the most satisfying parts of life can become the most divisive. This fact is apparent in my practice and Second Wives Club support groups time and time again. Individuals become entrenched with their friends and sometimes very possessive of them. Divorced couples tend to use their friends as pawns—as they do with children—and may barter for the continuation and fidelity of the friendship. But this bartering may have the subversive effect of disrupting the second wife's relationship with her spouse.

Please take the following quiz to help you assess the impact of friends' influences on your marriage.

♛ U I Z

Mark T for "true" and F for "false," and remember that honesty is the best you-know-what!

_____ 1. My husband's former wife's girlfriend calls him weekly to "keep in touch." He sees no harm in this, but I do.

_____ 2. My husband and I vacation spontaneously. His former wife always knows our destination, knowledge had by only my husband's "best friends" and us.

_____ 3. My spouse's best man at his first wedding refused that honor at our wedding, giving the excuse that he had been fond of the first wife. My husband feels hurt and wants to discontinue the relationship.

_____ 4. My husband has weekly bowling games with male friends from his former marriage.

_____ 5. Friends from my husband's past marriage try to include us in their social activities.

_____ 6. I feel extremely comfortable in the company of friends from my husband's prior marriage.

_____ 7. One of my husband's friends is his former brother-in-law. We often are in conflict about this relationship. I can't feel relaxed around this particular friend.

_____ 8. My husband should not continue attending birthday parties of children of "former" friends.

C H E C K L I S T

1. If you answered "true" to this statement, you are right on target! Generally speaking, it is questionable why a spouse's ex-wife's girlfriend should be so intent on continuing a friendship (or acquaintanceship) that is null and void. Furthermore, one must wonder why your husband wants to maintain a connection of this kind. Such a connection may be a signal of your husband's inability to let go of his former wife. This problem may originate in your spouse's unconscious and be allowed to manifest by way of "harmless" conversations with the ex-wife's girlfriend. Gently introduce these ideas to your husband so that he can explore their possibility. Let him know that you feel very uncomfortable about the situation and would like it to stop.

2. Of course, former marital partners should be able to contact each other when children are involved. (This can be accomplished via beepers, answering machines, or a mutual friend who holds the vacation destination in confidence.) If this is not applicable and you responded "true," a problem is evident. This may be a conflict of loyalty on the part of the "best friend." Sometimes friends of the former wife and your

husband find themselves in such turmoil that they are confused about their new role—friends of the former couple or the new couple? Your husband should inform his friends that his former wife was privy to information concerning vacations that only the friends were apprised of. This statement can be couched in terms of your husband holding the friendship dear to him but also needing the friends to respect his privacy and honor loyalty to him. In that way, your husband would be acknowledging his friends' confusion of divided loyalty and keeping the door open for the friendship to continue. Old friendships are to be treasured whenever possible.

3. If your husband's first best man refuses to serve at your wedding, perhaps he is giving your husband the message that their friendship is being compromised by his choice of wife (you). Encourage him to speak openly to his friends about this rather than terminate the relationship. We go through many hurts during a relationship, but getting past these hurts often results in stronger bonds. Discontinuation of a friendship is an extreme resolution of a conflict and could be a metaphor for other relationships of your husband's. This situation could be used as a learning process.

4. This is a tricky issue. You certainly want your husband to continue seeing male friends who have been an important source of support and fun to him. As we've stated, friendships do not necessarily have to be abandoned along with the prior marriage. But if your spouse's friends are also friends of his former wife, conflicts centering on ambiguous loyalty may

emerge. If you feel comfortable with this situation, let it continue. The time to discuss this with your mate is when and if you feel that friendship boundaries overlap with friends' marital boundaries. Remember, your goal as second wife is to remain LOVERS for life. Each component of LOVERS may be challenged in pursuit of your goal.

5. Many second wives would decline such social invitations. Every situation is different, but you and your spouse probably will feel awkward in such a clime. After all, you are the new kid on the block, which is seldom a comfortable place to be. Speak openly to your husband about these invitations and how to handle them. If he insists on socializing with his group of friends, perhaps he could do it with the husbands alone.

6. How fortunate for you and your mate that you are able to enjoy the company of "their" friends. If you responded positively to this statement and this is truly how you feel, it is to your credit. But if you responded "false" to this, don't be hard on yourself. It is normal and natural to display uneasiness in a somewhat questionable predicament. Help your spouse to understand your discomfort when this problem comes up.

7. If you responded "true" to this statement, it could potentially escalate into a major dispute between you and your husband. Your insistence that your spouse break off the friendship may cause resentment on his part. However precious friendships are, they are not worth the rifts they may cause in your marriage! The boundary between friend and former brother-in-law may be a very delicate one, but it is one that is possible to

navigate. Your husband will have to take responsibility not to sacrifice the trust and loyalty inherent in a good marriage in order to continue the friendship of his former brother-in-law. Should he be able to mastermind this dual loyalty successfully, it would be wise to limit the contacts in order not to compromise the fragile boundary. This cross between a good friend and a former relative is not a pretty place to be. Help your mate to become aware of the *Loyalty* component of LOVERS and its significance to your marital relationship. Of course, you need not be in the company of your husband's friend, so your level of comfort is not in question in that sense.

8. A response of "true" would infer that your spouse wants to attend such parties. You may question the motivations behind this desire. If he is particularly close to the children of "their" friends, other arrangements can be made to see them. But participating in an event where it is likely that your mate's former wife will be present is not in the best interest of the marriage. Here, again, the problem of divided loyalties becoming a divisive factor in your marriage underscores the importance of the *Loyalty* component of LOVERS. Without *Loyalty, Stability of Commitment* and *Value of Trust* in a marriage are also challenged.

More frequently than one might imagine, the circle of friends of a former relationship becomes intertwined with friends of a current relationship. You may encounter this predicament in your everyday life in a variety of milieus, including social, work, educational, and religious settings. Use the secrets from the Second Wives Club to handle the complications resulting from potentially sensitive encounters.

Let's examine the case of Joanne and Ted, a couple in their mid-twenties who had been married for one year. Both had had brief marriages right after high school. They had been acquainted for many years in their small town, although they had never dated. Shortly after their divorces, Joanne and Ted met again at a Regional YMCA party and soon began a courtship, which culminated in marriage. Joanne and her former husband had enjoyed an active social life, centering on the Y to which they and their families had belonged all their lives. The Y was their anchor in an otherwise chaotic existence fraught with family, financial, and drug problems. Joanne contributed to the Y by coordinating teenage activities. All of the couple's friends were members of the Y. Concurrently, Ted and his former wife also were members of the same Y. Each couple had its own circle of friends, with surprisingly little overlap.

The respective friends of both couples appeared to be supportive when they separated and eventually divorced. Both Joanne's and Ted's former spouses accepted jobs in other areas of the state, so their presence at Y functions was not an issue. Each circle of friends continued to embrace the remaining member of the couple. Both Joanne and Ted were able to benefit from the stability of the friendships during their fragile post-divorce periods. For the most part, their friends encouraged and applauded when Ted and Joanne married.

Problems ensued between Joanne and Ted when Y functions brought together the two circles of friends. A few friends of Ted's former wife greatly resented Joanne, saying that she was the "other woman" in Ted's first marriage and that she was an inappropriate role model for their teenagers. They tried to have her dismissed from her volunteer job. Joanne felt the brunt of their hostility repeatedly. Sometimes it was overt and other times passive. Nonetheless, the reality of this hostility made its impact on Joanne and Ted, causing them much consternation and leading to both sadness and arguments between them. Joanne sought membership in the Second Wives Club following a request from the Y president that she resign. At this low point in their marriage, they decided to seek objective assistance from a professional therapist.

DR. M.: From our conversation in the beginning of the session, it seems that you both are eager to confront the negative developments in your marriage. And you want to move on. You've stated that you're happy with one another but find that outside forces are making it difficult for you to communicate without bickering. You, Ted, have said that you feel as if you're being pulled in two directions—one toward your wife and the other toward your friends. Can you please elaborate on this?

TED: Dr. Millian, let me back up a little by saying that when my first wife, Wendy, and I were still married, we both knew Joanne because of her work with the teenagers at our Y. My kid brother was in Joanne's program and I often gave him rides to the Y. I admired Joanne's efforts with the kids, but it was nothing more than that. From time to time, Joanne and I had discussions about my brother because he was the kind of kid who seemed to get into trouble with the other kids. She tried to help him, and for that I was grateful. I didn't realize it then, but evidently some people were noticing our conversations. Even though we never saw each other outside the Y, we were being observed. Wendy and I separated and divorced simply because we fell out of love—this had nothing to do with Joanne in the least.

JOANNE: You're right, Ted. Your divorce and my divorce came about for entirely different reasons and had nothing to do with our knowing each other. I thought that our friends would always be there for us. Some were—but was I ever wrong about the others. Some of Ted's friends were out for blood—my blood! They smeared my name all over the Y, and even the little town we live in. And then they told the president of the Y to get rid of me because I was a bad influence on their kids. That was too much!

DR. M.: Did the president use those words to you, Joanne?

JOANNE: No, he didn't. He talked *around* the words, saying that although I wasn't being accused of cheating on my husband and breaking up another woman's marriage, there are certain people in the Y who feel that my relationship with Ted was a factor in his divorce. I always liked Ted, and our conversations weren't always about his kid brother, but we *never* were unfaithful to our spouses. It's just not true! We were two people in unhappy marriages that got a kick out of talking to each other. It was purely harmless!

TED: And here we are, still going to the Y because it is a part of our lives and has been for some time. Why should we quit the Y just because of some mean-spirited "friends"? I don't want to do that, but Joanne does because she feels humiliated. If this comes between us, then these people will have gotten what they want!

DR. M.: It is apparent that these jabs at your morality, Joanne, have stressed you out and led to much hurt. Furthermore, they've caused a rift in your relationship with Ted. What would you like to see happen in this case?

JOANNE: I don't want to leave the Y and don't want to leave the teenagers in the program. It's not fair! But I know that I can't take it anymore. Ted wants us to continue at the Y and hold our heads up high.

TED: We *should* hold our heads high, Joanne, because we've done nothing wrong. These people are wrong. Why should we resign from the Y? What do *you* think, Dr. Millian?

DR. M.: Of course, you've done nothing wrong. You've done nothing except to seek and find happiness in one another. However, people see what they want to see and think what they want to think. In the short run, it would be a great idea if each of you learned and used the Progressive Muscle Relaxation Exercise (see chapter 11) to help you handle the terrible stress the situation has put you under. In the long run, however, you both have to make the decision as to whether you want to subject yourselves continuously to the undercurrents of a hostile environment. Your attendance at Y functions should bring you joy, not aggravation. It should enhance living in your community. Perhaps it might be a good idea to see your faithful friends outside the Y, away from the rumormongers. Life is not fair, and you may have to view this conflict as a prime example of this principle.

The progressive muscle relaxation technique offered Ted and Joanne the respite they needed to distance themselves from the problem. It didn't change the situation, but it became a powerful behavioral tool against stress. Because of this technique, the couple was able to observe their plight in a more objective manner, and they decided to leave the Y and join another community club. The best intentions of friends can be toxic, but the couple didn't permit this to happen.

Which elements of **LOVERS** do you think that Joanne and Ted enjoyed in their marriage? How would you evaluate them? The conflict borne by their marriage seemed to strengthen them as a couple, and every component of **LOVERS** was working with the other. More important than excising the Y from their lives, these partners excised the challenges that could have potentially damaged their marriage.

Although this story took place in a community-club setting, the intertwining of two individual's friends can happen anywhere. If you feel that you are in an uncomfortable situation, it's probably because you *are* in one. Take a lesson from Joanne and discuss it with your husband. You must take control and not permit yourself or your marriage to be challenged because of unhappy friends.

Quite the opposite from the above (but nonetheless so powerful that it is palpable) is the scenario of a second wife finding herself becoming the "best friend" of a friend of her husband's former wife. This was the case with Jose and Elsa, who were thirty-two and twenty-seven years old, respectively, and had been married for over six years.

In brief, Angie was a good friend of Jose and his former wife, Mary. Angie spoke strongly to Jose and Mary about her love for each of them and said that she would let nothing get in the way of their friendship, not even their divorce. Angie was true to her word and went to great lengths to continue the friendships. It seemed to Elsa that this friend's efforts in cultivating her friendship with Jose exceeded the norm. Elsa reached the point where she questioned the motivations of Angie in pursuance of the three friendships and sometimes found Angie's tactics questionable. In truth, Angie took pains to honor any confidences gained from being a friend to Elsa, Mary, and Jose; she seemed to take delight in being a "true" friend to all three. She was a kind and spiritual person with no ulterior motive except to be a good friend.

Elsa never had experienced a person who so wanted to befriend her in such a way. She had difficulty socially in her personal relationships and felt overwhelmed with Angie's persistence and closeness. Elsa's reaction was to jump back from Angie and to feel threatened by her desire to become "best friends." Elsa also wondered whether Angie's motivation in becoming her friend was to report back to Jose's first wife, Mary.

This challenge presented by a friend stemmed not from reality but from the inner workings of Elsa's mind. Elsa's low self-esteem and inadequate social skills eventuated in her false suspicions about a woman whose needs were purely and simply—although perhaps naïvely—just to be a friend to all. A distraught Elsa called me just to "talk things over—nothing long term." She was seen in individual counseling and, over time, was helped to come to grips with the situation.

Her therapy had a three-fold approach. First, we addressed self-esteem issues in order to improve her feelings about herself. It was helpful for her to make a list of her positive attributes. When one sees such a list in black-and-white, one can more freely appreciate one's finer qualities, and feel better about oneself.

Second, I suggested that Elsa enter a small group for a period of time. This helped Elsa improve her interpersonal skills and proved to be a valuable aid in developing these talents.

Third, I asked both Elsa and Jose to enter marital counseling in order to help them remain LOVERS for life. Each component of

LOVERS was worked on, and having the couple role-play various scenarios seemed to be a helpful aid in illustrating this vital concept.

As you can see from this story, Elsa's fears were of her own doing. We must become aware of our weaknesses as well as our assets and examine ourselves for any part they may play in destroying our partnerships. We need to remember to refer to the LOVERS concept and have the support of the Second Wives Club to help us through these challenges. Try to learn from Elsa—assess, evaluate, and step back from the problem in order to go forward.

EIGHT

Challenge Number Six: The Ashes of Time

(THE SMOLDERING MEMORIES)

WE ALL RECOGNIZE THAT ONE of the most precious commodities on our earth is time. Time can work for us or against us. It is said that the hottest coals dwindle down to the coolest, flickering embers still capable of reigniting whatever they touch. Who among us has not tempted our senses—and our fate—by once again exploring the same territory in which we found joy in other times and with other people? And by exposing our eyes and ears to similar titillations we treasured in the past? Yes, individuals from another time in our lives were there to share our moments of ecstasy. Sometimes the ambiguity and anguish not only are at odds with the present but also are too difficult to give up. We may yearn unconsciously for that which was, even though it is imbued with pain. Our significant other of today probably is unable to understand why he hangs on to the past in ways that are self-destructive. Indeed, we, ourselves, cannot understand this paradox. But we make excuses to keep the threads of the past in our present lives, even at the cost of the relationships of today. Why does this happen? Why do we shoot ourselves in the foot?

Emily and Harry serve as a case in point from my practice. Many months after the breakup of Harry's marriage to Donna and his hasty exit from their house, he made arrangements to retrieve his clothing and personal effects. Harry returned to his apartment laden with his belongings, including several cartons of photographs. Donna had placed the cartons in strategic spots—adjacent to suits, in underwear drawers, and on Harry's desk. At the time, Harry could have chosen not to take the cartons. It was evident, however, that he was unable to make the decision to intentionally sever the visual cord binding Donna and him. He thought, "There may be pictures of my family in those cartons."

Harry's tiny apartment had no space in which to store the photos. He placed them in the living room with the other memorabilia so that he could examine the contents at leisure. Emily was distraught upon encountering the cartons but at first said nothing to her then-fiancé. She assumed that Harry would dispose of the cartons promptly. Three weeks had passed when Emily confronted Harry with the distress she was experiencing because of the continued presence of the photos in the apartment. She felt hurt by Harry's insensitivity to her feelings regarding the pictures. She imagined an "evil, strangulating hold" on Harry, an obstacle to his going forward in his life with her.

Emily and Harry sought counseling because of the subsequent strain on their relationship stemming from Harry's attachment to the photos and reluctance to dispose of them. In counseling, both were given behavior-modification techniques such as Thought Stopping. Emily became a Second Wives Club member and learned to use the progressive muscle relaxation technique (see chapter 11) to help control her overreactions and back off from Harry. These were used as stopgaps to get them through the crisis.

Although the general thrust of the counseling was aimed at Harry's persistence in holding on to the photos of his prior marriage, other issues had to be addressed as well. An important dynamic in their turmoil pertained to Emily herself. Due to many factors in her background, Emily harbored feelings of insecurity toward men deep within herself. These feelings were rooted in her unconscious and, therefore, out of her awareness. Nonetheless, they were real and they were instrumental in recalling and projecting distrust onto Harry. Emily had a history of being burdened with gnawing jealousy and paranoia toward men. Harry, of course, was no exception.

The partners agreed to come into counseling individually so that they could reach healthier places in their emotional lives.

Over time, Emily was able not only to understand her feelings in the context of their destructive nature, but to put them aside. Eventually, Emily was able to release the grip of uncertainty and move on. Her progress in healing her vulnerable emotions with regard to men, together with her retreat from the volatile marital situation, was effective. That is, Emily was able to step back from the minefield in which she had found herself and offer Harry the time he needed to discover why he was unable to let go of the memories from Donna. Harry needed to work through and resolve the true underlying dynamics of the problem.

DR. M.: Harry, in the beginning of our sessions, you spoke of a very tumultuous association with your first wife, Donna. You said that the first few years of your marriage were wonderful, romantic, and the dream relationship you always had envisioned for yourself. Why were you initially drawn to Donna? Can you explain it?

HARRY: My answer is going to seem as shallow as I feel, and I hope you'll understand and not be bored by what I have to say. Donna captivated me because of her good looks. Girls didn't like me—in school they didn't pay attention to me and I couldn't get a date. Maybe it was because of my weight! I was always so skinny and gaunt-looking that I felt ugly with a capital *U*. I was desperate to get a girl's attention. Once in a while, I'd get it, but it would be from the "wrong" girl—either someone equally "ugly" or another type of loser. That's the way I felt about myself—a loser.

DR. M.: Harry, it's a sad way to grow up thinking of yourself as someone unworthy of love and understanding from another. Since we all are prisoners of our own minds, your negative self-image really set you up for disappointments and heartaches.

HARRY: Thanks for understanding and for listening. You asked why I was attracted to Donna. Number one, she seemed interested in me, and number two, she was extremely pretty. Can you imagine— a pretty girl who was willing to go out with me? She really wanted to spend a lot of time with me. She said she wasn't bored with me. And she hung on my every word. What a combination!

DR. M.: If things went so well between the two of you, what happened to lead to the downfall of your marriage? It's helpful for you to learn from your past relationship so that any mistakes won't be repeated in the present or the future.

HARRY: I'm sure you've heard this again and again—and I don't want you to go out of your mind with my monotonous story. Are you sure you want to listen to this?

DR. M.: Harry, you seem to be saying over and over that what you talk about is not worthy of my time. You've thanked me for understanding you and for listening to you. Perhaps what you are saying is that you've not had experiences in which you're understood. And perhaps you feel as if you've not been listened to.

HARRY: I don't know. . . . I'll have to think about that. Surely, *you* as my counselor listen to me and try hard to understand me.

DR. M.: Yes, Harry, but please keep in mind that the way you relate to individuals in the world outside my office is the way you relate to me inside the office. You don't check your personality at the door. So we can learn a lot from the way you perceive me. Though I truly am interested in learning about you and therefore I listen attentively to you, it's normal and natural for you to think I'm not interested, not understanding, and not listening. This has been your experience in relating to others.

HARRY: That makes a lot of sense. And that relates to what happened with Donna. In the beginning of our relationship, she actually listened to me. I couldn't get over it. And this woman who listened to me was also beautiful! How could I resist? Now I understand the power Donna had over me!

DR. M.: I'm impressed that you're able to gain so much insight from our conversations. Because of your ability, your prognosis is favorable. But let's get on to my question of what went wrong with your marriage.

HARRY: After we married, Donna stopped listening to me—she turned me off. She didn't say so at first, but I could see that she was becoming less and less interested in what I had to say. I spoke to her about it and she denied it, but I knew that it was true. She started to work extremely long hours, saying that her boss needed her. And then she had to make trips away on business. Since when does an administrative secretary have to accompany her boss on exotic trips? Again, Donna denied any loss of interest in me. She claimed over and over again that she was fascinated by her job, and that she wanted to carve out a career niche for herself in the company. Finally, she told me that she was in love with her boss and that she wanted a divorce from me. It was a horrible scene. There went my pretty wife; there went my life.

DR. M.: Harry, the only woman who paid you the attention you sought in order to feel good about yourself rejected you. What a tragic and difficult time it was for you in your life! You had sought validation of yourself as a worthy man through marrying an attractive and attentive woman. But that didn't work! And it never really works out, because a person who enters a relationship to fill a void in himself or herself is committing a self-imposed injustice. Such an association is built upon need. A healthy relationship foundation must be constructed on free choice, not on need.

Harry agreed that his low self-esteem was getting in the way of having fruitful and adult relationships with women, particularly Emily. Throughout the many sessions that followed, Harry and I worked toward the goal of helping him increase the value he placed upon himself. While this took time, therapy eventually got to the point where the presenting problem (the reason that brought him into therapy) was reintroduced.

DR. M.: Harry, it puzzles me that you would want to hold onto objects and photos of yourself and Donna. You were rejected and hurt by your first wife. I haven't noticed that you have masochistic tendencies. Surely, there must be other reasons.

HARRY: Actually, Dr. Millian, until now I really didn't think I was holding on to the photos for any purpose except to cull through them. I thought there might be pictures of my parents and other members of my family scattered among the photos. Now, after speaking with you about my needs and the kind of person I had been most of my life, I'm questioning my motives. What stopped me from tossing away the photos? Here I have a great marriage with Emily and have everything going for me. Why is it so hard to chuck those snapshots?

DR. M.: Harry, I think basically the difficulty lies in the importance you placed upon Donna to help you feel valuable as a person. Having her as a wife was a pivotal time in your emotional development because you felt worthwhile—but for all the wrong reasons. The photos you shared with Donna captured the good times, the times you felt on top of the world—your world. It was hard enough for you to let go of that feeling when she asked for a divorce. But then you had a double whammy when you were confronted with disposing of those photos. It was like reliving the agony of her rejection, and it brought home the cruel reality of the situation. You had to face the demise of your relationship all over again, in spite of the new woman in your life—Emily. Harry, your difficulty in discarding the photos reflected your need to retain some relationship, any relationship, with the first woman who listened and understood you. This was not in your awareness. You acted out of an unconscious need. It's totally understandable—but totally destructive.

Eventually, Harry culled through the photos, discarding those that were only reiterating lingering memories of his ex-wife. This helped him bring closure to the marriage with Donna—a critical phase needed to open a future with Emily. This story of a Second Wives Club member clearly demonstrates the impact of the reigniting embers of visual memories and the "wildfire" damage caused by them. Photographs can be key visual triggers to a past relationship. In a remarriage, even the mere disposition of photos can be fraught with pain and agony. Should your husband be reluctant to dispose of old photos or even insist on retaining them ("They're just pictures, honey"), you might question his inability to let go. This behavior might imply that he left his hopes and dreams with her, and all that remains are his precious photos. In turn, this might suggest to you that your love together is not enough, compromising the quality of your marriage. You may feel that the photos are like weapons, shooting holes in your efforts to build a strong and vital union.

Memories can be jack-in-the-boxes ready to pop holes in your relationships. Are they *your* jack-in-the-box? If so, consider taking positive action, as did Harry and Emily.

Please take the following quiz to help you determine if memories are smoldering sufficiently to ignite, with a negative impact.

Mark T *for "true" and* F *for "false."*

_____ 1. My husband sometimes confuses "their" favorite song with ours.

_____ 2. My spouse appears to be uncomfortable viewing films in which a couple divorces.

_____ 3. My husband's ex-wife collected antique paperweights. I've noticed that he quickly moves past such objects when we browse in antique shops.

_____ 4. Surely, my spouse and his former wife have shared memories, but he has not mentioned a single one.

_____ 5. My husband becomes unusually quiet when we picnic near a lake, even though we are more than five hundred miles from the lake house he and his former wife shared.

_____ 6. Having sex in locations other than bed was favored by my partner and his ex. He freaks out when I don't go along with what "they" preferred.

_____ 7. When I order red wine rather than white, my husband becomes agitated. Although he denies any connection between red wine and his former wife, her insistence on red wine was well known to our mutual friends.

_____ 8. My husband insists on keeping his easy chair from his first marriage.

1. The key word here is *sometimes.* If your favorite song (color, book, flowers, etc.) occasionally becomes mixed up with "hers," it is acceptable, particularly if your husband's first marriage was of long duration and your relationship with him is rather young. This is because long associations, by definition, are difficult to sever. For example, to disconnect *mother and apple pie, ham and cheese,* or *black and white* would be challenging. Research points to a psychological phenomenon called *conditioning* in which a pairing of long association becomes unconsciously entrenched in one's mind. Therefore, you can understand that a favorite song of long duration becomes part of one's unconscious association of *song* and *favorite.* If this occurs in your marriage, speak gently to your husband about it to remind him of *your* favorite song. Remember, long associations are habits and are hard to break. Patience is needed!

2. If your husband is uncomfortable with films mentioning divorce, it may indicate that your husband still has feelings about the marriage and/or the divorce. Don't despair. These feelings may not necessarily imply love for the ex-wife or regret over divorce. Perhaps your spouse was raised in a religion in which divorce was not sanctioned. Or perhaps he feels enormous guilt over the divorce for reasons other than the marriage being unhappy for both. No matter what ignites the spark for his apparent discomfort, please recognize that your partner is entitled to his feelings and that time should

help ease his way. Unless this dilemma persists for years, it would not bode well for you to let the situation evolve into a bigger issue.

3. Here, too, is evidence of the power of association, although it may not be purely unconscious in this case. Your mate simply may not like the memory of his ex evoked by the visible symbol of her passion for paperweights. After all, one's predilection for a particular collectible is intimately connected to one's identity and personality. Antique shops contain a myriad of objects; your spouse need not attend to the paperweights if he chooses not to. In other words, please don't create a problem if there isn't one.

4. Let's face facts: A successful second marriage does not depend in any way on a spouse revealing memories of a first marriage. Shared memories of a relationship gone sour usually are imbued with pain. It doesn't make sense to bring up such memories. A second wife may feel that her husband is being secretive—but what's the point? Note the *Value of Trust* element in **LOVERS** and let that be the keynote of your situation.

5. If you responded "true" to this statement, your husband may likely have a painful association that prohibits an enjoyable picnic with you at a lake. It doesn't matter if the lake house he and his first wife had was five miles, five hundred miles, or five thousand miles from the current lake location. Psychic (mind) connections know no distance. They are powerful associations! Although your husband may be enthusiastic

about picnicking with you at a lake, perhaps this is not the time to go. The decision ultimately depends on the interval of time between the two relationships. A shorter period of time between relationships, understandably, evokes a stronger association than a longer period of time. If an association still brings up pain and discomfort after many years, it points to problems. Discussions aimed at helping your spouse understand the significance of the painful association would be a first step. Looking into your marital relationship by speaking to an objective professional clearly would be a much-needed second step. Your goal is to be LOVERS for life, and this is accomplished by clarifying the stumbling blocks and not letting them become obstacles.

6. Responding "true" to this statement is another indication of the "three in a bed" problem. Habits become established over time and become entrenched in one's mind as preferences. Sexual habits are no different from any others in this sense. Your husband may have found having sex any place other than bed to be a powerful turn-on, and become dependent on it. For you to go along with your husband may feel like having the ghostly intrusion of his former wife in *your* bed. Not a good thing! This is where the *Empathy* and *Openness* components of LOVERS reaches an even higher level of importance. Paradoxically, sex seems to be an area in which many partners have difficulty in being frank and forthcoming. Should sex prove too challenging for you and your spouse to discuss, professional help is an option. Remember,

as many Second Wives Club members attest, practicing being **LOVERS** will also help nurture your physical relationship with the man you love.

7. Associations with food and drink tend to be exceedingly powerful forces in one's psyche. For example, if you eat something that gives you food poisoning, you are going to have an aversion to that food for a long time. Conversely, food or drink that evokes pleasant memories is likely to be favorable until such time as it brings up anxiety or hurt. If you responded "true" to this statement, the association of red wine with the former wife is probably painful for your husband. Again, the strength of this association depends on the amount of time between relationships. Remember that these associations stem from the unconscious and, therefore, depend on it for coming into awareness. Talk to your husband about this and help him to make a new and happy association between you, his second wife, and your pleasure in drinking red wine. Don't let connections with food or drink deteriorate into minefields!

8. People become attached to extremely comfortable furniture, and a response of "true" to this statement places your husband into this category. To you, the easy chair may seem to be a symbol of his first marriage, an undesirable icon of a time gone by. While it isn't a monumental obstruction in the course of your marriage, what the chair represents is discomforting for you. Let your spouse understand your thoughts on this matter, and suggest that you both shop for another easy

chair. If he is insistent on the original easy chair, you might ask him to be more sensitive to your needs. This visible memory might give you motivation to seek professional help to learn to remain **LOVERS** for life.

Vacations are another modality often imbued with memories that can wreak havoc in the very soul of a marriage. Barbara and Justin, ages forty-four and thirty-nine, honeymooned in Spain at his suggestion. Discussions had ensued between the couple concerning the choice of Spain, particularly the city of Madrid. Justin had taken his former wife, Jill, to that city, enjoying its splendors many times. He wanted to share his joy with Barbara. In Madrid, restaurants, hotels, museums, and streets were fleshed out with memories from Justin's former marriage. Barbara felt that her honeymoon had been shared by a third person, absent only in a physical sense.

Justin and Barbara returned from their honeymoon in a state of panic. Nothing had gone well. Justin felt angry that Barbara did not appreciate the joys of a magnificent city. Justin's endeavors to share his knowledge of the wonders of Madrid were interpreted by Barbara as a subversive vehicle in which to keep Jill in the picture. The fledgling marriage was imperiled.

Several weeks after their return from Madrid, Barbara and Justin yielded to the unrelenting strain between them and phoned for an initial professional consultation. It was then that Barbara revealed her initial reluctance to marry. Her parents had endured a lengthy marriage characterized by severe verbal abuse. Both parents had self-medicated with drugs and alcohol in order to tolerate their relationship. Obviously, the chemical substances masked Barbara's parent's deeper conflicts.

DR. M.: Barbara and Justin, it's impressive that you are willing to get professional help so early on in the marriage, but also very sad. From what you both said before, you love each other and want your marriage to prosper. Barbara, you waited until the age of forty-four to marry for the first time. Justin, your first marriage ended unhappily in divorce, and at the age of thirty-nine, you knew the kind of woman you wanted. Let's try to see what's gone wrong. Who would like to begin? This is always the hardest part of the session.

BARBARA: OK, Dr. Millian, you mentioned my age and that I waited so long to marry. Sure, I waited—who wouldn't, in my circumstances? As a kid living at home, I was in a constant state of chaos. I never knew from one day to another what my life would be like. My parents were drunks and drug addicts. What a combination! We lived from hand to mouth, on assistance from the state, and from family members who took pity on us. I could never bring friends home— it was a mess!

DR. M.: It's truly amazing, Barbara, that you lifted yourself out of the life into which you were born, into your present life.

JUSTIN: Pretty spectacular person, wouldn't you say?

BARBARA: It wasn't easy. I was determined to get out of the miserable existence my parents called life and to rise above it. I studied, got college scholarships, and worked my butt off. Then I became an accountant, and a successful one at that! I did well financially and fulfilled my dream of not having to depend on anyone, anytime, anywhere.

DR. M.: It seems that you worked hard to attain financial independence. How about emotional independence?

BARBARA: That was easy. My theory was that if I don't become emotionally involved with a guy, I'm independent in that way too. No man, no problem, no pain.

DR. M.: Your reluctance to establish relationships is understandable, Barbara. However, in the process of protecting yourself from hurt, perhaps you inadvertently robbed yourself of the loving harmony of a human relationship. You said that even when Justin came into your life, you hesitated to become entangled with him. You said you were frightened of the intimacy of such a relationship. However, despite your reluctance to marry anyone, you married Justin. What changed your mind?

JUSTIN: If I could interrupt here—I changed her mind. I loved Barbara more than I had ever loved anyone before. I knew about her background; I knew her past relationships with men were sporadic and superficial. I wanted to show her what love could really be like. I wanted to show her the world. I wanted to give her what she deserved!

BARBARA: Dr. Millian, how could I resist a man like Justin? He offered me friendship and love; he offered me a life I never thought existed with another person.

DR. M.: From what you both are saying, you had the highest hopes for your marriage, but then the hopes were dashed at your honeymoon. Do you recall how the decision was made to honeymoon in Madrid?

JUSTIN: Actually, I travel quite extensively on business, and one of my favorite cities in the world is Madrid. I love that city to the point of vacationing there whenever possible, because it offers so much, day and night. I told Barbara about Madrid and what great times I've had there. I wanted Barbara to enjoy that city the same way I had enjoyed it.

DR. M.: Had you discussed Madrid in terms of having gone there many times with your ex-wife, Jill?

BARBARA: Oh yes, I knew that Jill and Justin had been to Madrid many times, and it didn't even pass my mind that there would be a problem there.

DR. M.: It might be, Barbara, that you weren't really tuned in to your true feelings or how it would affect you to go to the city where Justin had vacationed frequently with Jill. Perhaps you did such a good job in detaching yourself from meaningful relationships that you didn't realize it would really bother you to be in a place where your husband had found pleasures with another woman. Unconsciously, it might be that you had built a characterological wall around yourself, like a suit of armor. The wall prevented you from getting hurt, and the wall prevented you from becoming sensitive to your own needs and desires. In other words, the nuances of life were not in your awareness. Being in Madrid was like tearing down the wall for you—so healthy but so hurtful!

The couple attended a number of marital counseling sessions in which they became aware of the deleterious effect of the subtle influence of vacations revisited. They were urged to practice the LOVERS concept of a healthy relationship. After integrating the components of LOVERS into their daily lives, their marriage prospered.

As you can see from the case of Barbara and Justin, past marriage memories can act as a jack-in-the-box by popping up to disturb your relationship when you least expect it. A marriage is a cumulative collection of time stored in one's conscious and unconscious memories either as treasures or traumas, as good times or bad times. The vast and inclusive memories of shared life take many forms, including photographs, songs, books, vacations, restaurants, money, sex, and so forth, which easily can become influences that may put a marriage in peril. Being LOVERS in your marriage can help to overcome these lingering memories. And when you disempower the memories, you will become a successful member of the Second Wives Club.

The impact of smoldering memories in the unconscious mind can also take the form of symbolic jewelry. The following scenario many seem absurd to you, but read on to learn how a Second Wives Club member coped with her young marriage.

Lynn and Tom were in their early twenties when they decided to become engaged. Ordinarily, agreeing to tie the knot means the purchase of a ring to commemorate the event. The ring, therefore, becomes a symbol of the engagement and is viewed as sacred to that commitment. Tom had a previous marriage in his late teens. He and his family had designed a ring especially for Tom's first wife, Connie. His parents generously had Connie select a diamond wristwatch as an engagement gift from themselves and as a token of their love for her.

Following the divorce, both pieces of jewelry were returned to Tom and kept in the family safe-deposit box. Tom gave these beautiful pieces of jewelry to Lynn upon their engagement. Lynn said that she loved the ring and the watch; both were more elegant than she could have imagined herself to own.

Shortly thereafter, Tom told Lynn that the jewelry had been worn by his ex-wife, Connie. There was nothing malicious in this act—the jewelry was there for Tom's use, and use it he did, for his fiancé. Lynn was devastated. She felt insulted by Tom and his family, and was very hurt that she had been gifted with "recycled" symbols of Tom's love for another woman. Lynn decided to avoid confrontation and say nothing about the situation. She wore the ring and the watch without comment. The smoldering memories took the form of this jewelry tainted by another wife, another marriage. What more prominent reminder of a first wife could there be but a symbol of love in diamonds? The jewels symbolized Tom's past and represented the hurt Lynn felt at not receiving special gifts from Tom and his parents. Lynn's dismay and her sullen, quiet acceptance of the relics indicated her need to become a practicing member of the Second Wives Club.

Lynn stored the ring and watch not in a safe-deposit box but in a shoebox in her closet. One day, she decided to have a few pairs of shoes heeled. Lynn gave the shoe-repair person two boxes of her shoes—yes, including the box that contained the jewelry. She no longer wore the pieces; they were out of mind and out of sight, and she never saw the jewelry again. The power of the unconscious mind is so strong that it "willed" Lynn to rid herself of the jewelry, which was tantamount to ridding herself of Tom's ex-wife via the jewels.

This chapter has detailed some of the most contaminating memories of past marriages and the many ways in which they reignite and flare up. As a second wife, the many manifestations of lingering memories specific to you are loud and clear. Try to learn from the cases presented. Don't be afraid to use the behavioral techniques in chapter 11 if they are appropriate for you. Your goal is to remain LOVERS for life, and in order to walk that walk, you might need to illuminate the memories that are haunting your marriage. It's worth it!

Summary: Putting Your Life in Wonderful Perspective

SECOND WIVES, HERE ARE SOME general guidelines that you can apply to many situations. Let's review a few effective and powerful thoughts, attitudes, and skills that will release all those potential jack-in-the-boxes in your marriage—whether they take the form of your own needs, first wives, children, grandchildren, your mother-in-law, friends, or memories. These Second Wives Club secrets can help you remain LOVERS for life. Are you ready? Here we go . . .

It is best not to respond impulsively to any situation. Take the time to think things over slowly and carefully. Words and actions cannot be retracted or forgotten. If you have difficulty in this area, slow yourself down by withdrawing from situations temporarily, exercising, giving yourself time to unwind, and so forth. It's also a good idea to write down your thoughts and feelings on a large sheet of paper.

This will help you organize your thinking and clarify your feelings, so that you'll be more relaxed and calm enough to approach your situation clearly and rationally.

Stress is a part of our daily civilized lives. But you can learn to manage stress so that it will not be overwhelming and take its toll physically and mentally. One powerful technique that can help you reduce stress is the Progressive Muscle Relaxation Exercise (see chapter 11). This exercise teaches you how to relax your muscle groups one by one. The theory is that if you become as limp and loose as a rag doll, you can't remain tense and tight with stress. This stress-management technique can be learned by anyone. Less stress means a more relaxed you, and a more relaxed you means that you'll respond more calmly to an early warning sign of a challenging situation.

Communication skills are vital to any relationship. When you sense the subtle beginnings of a challenge, it is important to feel comfortable in raising the issue with your mate. You will feel more confident in your abilities to initiate a discussion if you have developed these skills. A simple lesson in improving your communication skills is offered in chapter 11. Dialogue between partners is imperative in any situation for a clear understanding of each other's feelings and thoughts. Competence in this aspect of a relationship is an effective response to any warning sign that a jack-in-the-box is about to pop!

Most of us recognize the steps necessary to grow a garden successfully. We can't merely plant the seedlings and expect them to grow unattended. These seedlings have to be watered, fertilized, weeded, and exposed to sunlight. Otherwise one ends up with nothing but weeds. Your relationship could be viewed as a garden. Gardens and marriages need the same loving care. Your relationship requires constant attention and cannot be taken for granted. It needs to be lovingly attended and cultivated. Each partner must work toward this goal and let the other know how special he or she is to the other. A special regard is the life force of a healthy relationship. It might be helpful for you and your husband to list the ways in which this special regard could be achieved by one another. (For example, "I feel special when he touches my arm.") Creating a special feeling is an effective response to a warning sign that a jack-in-the-box is about to pop up in your marriage. Challenges fade quickly when each person feels special to the other.

Sometimes it is difficult to pull yourself back from a situation and be objective. Objectivity is crucial. When one becomes enmeshed in a situation, bias sets in and distorts the picture. A professional counselor with experience in relationships can help a couple extricate themselves from a volatile situation and move on. A counselor can often be a pivotal force in the constructive healing of a marriage. A counselor can quickly analyze the problems in your marriage and guide you in the direction of an effective resolution. The particular problems that arise in a second marriage are sometimes hard to dislodge and require professional assistance. Should you feel that extra help is needed, contact your county mental-health association or a state psychological or social-work association, or ask your medical provider to recommend a licensed or certified mental-health professional. Be proud of yourself that you are smart enough to seek help when you need it!

The term *enlightened selfishness* (see chapter 6) was coined to describe a healthy state of mind in which the focus is on taking good care of yourself. This, of course, does not mean selfishness in the sense of being greedy, or exploiting others for your own satisfaction. It means only that you must act in your best interest in a knowing, enlightened manner. Taking this path will lead to the feeling that "all is right with the world." After all, if you keep giving to others without getting anything back, the well runs dry, leading to what we all recognize as "burnout." You might have discovered already that when you take care of your needs and wants and desires, you are far better able to take care of others. It may help if you conceptualize yourself as an extremely hungry waitress, impatiently and uncomfortably trying to attend to equally hungry customers. This waitress is unable to give her all to her work—because *she* is empty. Like you, her first responsibility is to herself, for the sake of herself. By taking care of her own needs (that is, feeding herself), this waitress is practicing *enlightened selfishness*. Try it on for size—you'll like it, I promise you!

After reading this book, second wife, I am certain that you understand the concept of LOVERS and are ready to join the successful members of the Second Wives Club. The acronym LOVERS was devised as an easy way to recall the key elements of a powerful and harmonious relationship. Things can become tough and challenging in your attempts to live life and resolve problems. Staying focused on remaining LOVERS for life, even in the midst of a tumultuous moment, can be the north star that guides you through.

The six components of LOVERS point to symmetry in a relationship—six is an even, balanced sum; no one component has more weight than another. Each component is necessary for the existence and health of the others. This is a useful metaphor for your marriage: symmetry and balance in your relationship are vital to one another. When the components are in harmony, you and your spouse will be able to forge a strong union capable of "defeating" any challenges that may occur in your marriage. Your strengths will help you sidestep any minefields that might be planted in the form of past histories. LOVERS is a relationship concept by which you can truly live a fulfilled, nurturing, and satisfying life together.

Throughout this book, the difficulties faced by second wives have been approached consistently in order to offer you a workable and productive framework for successful resolution. As you may have noted, the schema runs like this:

1. Awareness of the problem.

2. Defining the problem.

3. Applying solutions to the problem.

4. Short-term behavioral techniques, such as communication skills, relaxation methods, thought stopping, and assertiveness training.

5. Specific, usable relationship skills, such as enhanced communication and problem-solving.

6. Embracing the LOVERS concept as a constant, unifying factor in your marriage.

Step 1 is awareness of the problem. It is puzzling that many individuals become enmeshed in a situation that is unhappy and stressful. And yet, the more they are mired in the quicksand of the problem, the more they are unable to extricate themselves. They know that something is not right; they know that they are miserable—but they don't know why. In other words, they cannot isolate the dynamics of their difficulties enough to spell out the specifics of their trauma. It is hoped that through the quizzes, the stories from Second Wives Club members, and the self-diagnostic quiz in chapter 10, you will uncover your problem so that it can be addressed.

Step 2, defining the problem, goes a bit further than awareness of the problem. After becoming aware that something is not right, we still may be muddled. The reason for that confusion may be that we have not been able to zero in on the nitty-gritty of the conflict. We must make a collaborative effort to come up with a clear, exact definition of the nature of the problem, the parameters of the problem, and the effects of the problem on the relationship. It's important that both husband and wife be precise. Obviously, writing down the definition of the conflict is an aid toward understanding the thoughts and attitudes of the other. When the conflict is articulated on paper by both individuals, there is little room for misunderstandings.

Step 3 addresses some of the possible ways in which to come to a resolution of the conflict. The checklist sections in each chapter, plus insights gleaned from the stories, offer many ways in which to get past problems. The checklists are intended to supplement the case studies, but of course no list could pretend to be all-inclusive. The insights and remedies offered in the checklists are meant to stimulate your thinking in a positive and productive direction. Sometimes all that's needed is to give a second wife a good boost to get started and to believe in herself. Anything to help you become a practicing member of the Second Wives Club is welcomed at any point!

Step 4 carries great relevance for the second wife. When we are in control of our emotional selves, we can handle traumatic situations with aplomb. That is, we are less likely to overreact or to become distraught when jack-in-the-boxes surprise us if we, ourselves, are in charge. That's why it is so important to make good use of the short-term behavioral techniques presented in chapter 11. Your ability to utilize the long-term solutions is enhanced when you are in a more relaxed state of mind with sharp coping skills. Lack of patience with the problem-solving process is an impediment to your full membership in the Second Wives Club. You have everything to gain by practicing these techniques—and nothing to lose!

Step 5 concerns the skills needed to improve your relationship with your husband. In addition, please realize that these skills are invaluable for relating to everyone in your life. These are interpersonal skills at their best, and they will ease your way through life. Please take the time to read about them carefully, using role-playing whenever possible in order to integrate them into your everyday life. Misunderstanding frequently occurs between two individuals simply because their empathy skills are inadequate and they don't really listen to each other. Oftentimes, one partner is so busy thinking of a retort in their own mind that *real* listening and, therefore, *real* understanding become impossible. Keep in mind that our comprehension of someone's words often is subject to our own personal experiences and, as such, may be a distortion of the other's thoughts. It is best to paraphrase your partner's words in order to make certain that you have an accurate reflection of their thoughts.

There can't be too much said for the value of step 6—the concept of LOVERS. It is the cornerstone of all the other steps, and as implied earlier in this section, it is the heart of each chapter in this book. Please abide by it; please live it and breathe it, for it will stand you in good stead. You marry much more than just the man, and remaining LOVERS for life can be your key to success in the Second Wives Club.

The guidelines in this book will help you to make changes in your relationship with your husband on many levels. After all, you married for love, you married for keeps, you married to be LOVERS for life. Why stumble over the minefields thrown your way from your mate's first marriage? Why let smoldering memories hover over your kitchen and your bedroom? Problems have to be understood, not repeated. Solutions have to be implemented, not put aside. Your life, your love, your family have to be in a beautiful, harmonious balance—and in wonderful and glorious perspective. Our blessings to you all.

T E N

How to Find Your Challenge

FOR EACH OF THE STATEMENTS
in the following lists, assign a numerical value that best applies to
your feelings, using this scale:

1 **NEVER**

2 **RARELY**

3 **OCCASIONALLY**

4 **CONSTANTLY**

Write the appropriate number on the line before each statement.
At the end of each section, add up the numbers and write the total
score. Your score for each section indicates if you have a particular
problem in that area.

After you've completed each section, add all your subtotal scores.
This total is your cumulative score, which indicates the remedial
action needed to improve your marriage.

<u> 2 </u> My husband tells me he hates me. (Rarely)

<u> 3 </u> My husband tells me he can't stand my cooking. (Occasionally)

<u> 5 </u> Total

F O R M E R W I F E

<u>   </u>   1. My husband calls me by his ex-wife's name.

<u>   </u>   2. My husband spends time on the telephone talking to his ex-wife.

<u>   </u>   3. I question my husband's level of commitment to me.

<u>   </u>   4. I consider my husband to be generally unreliable.

<u>   </u>   5. I can trust my husband with my deepest secrets.

<u>   </u>   6. My husband talks about how difficult life is for his ex-wife.

<u>   </u>   7. In addition to alimony and child support, my husband still feels financially responsible for his ex-wife.

<u>   </u>   8. My husband still confuses her favorite foods with mine.

<u>   </u>   9. I am concerned that my husband has regrets about his divorce.

<u>   </u> 10. I feel that my love is not enough for my husband.

<u>   </u> Total

THEIR CHILDREN

_____ 1. My husband overextends himself to "their" children.

_____ 2. Although I want my husband to be a loving father, he puts "their" children before "ours."

_____ 3. My husband seems unable to say "no" to "their" children.

_____ 4. My husband is available at all times to "their" children regardless of our plans.

_____ 5. Situations in which "their" children take precedence occur often.

_____ 6. My husband favors time with "their" children over time with "ours."

_____ 7. My husband is more lenient with "their" children than with "ours."

_____ 8. "Their" children take advantage of my husband's continuous need to please them.

_____ 9. "Their" children act distant to me when they visit.

_____ 10. My husband does not include me in plans with "their" children.

_____ Total

GRANDCHILDREN

_____ 1. My husband's grandchildren take priority over "our" grandchildren.

_____ 2. My husband is overly generous with "their" grandchildren.

_____ 3. If a choice must be made between spending time with "their" grandchildren or with me, my husband chooses the grandchildren.

_____ 4. My grandchildren seem to be of little interest to my husband.

_____ 5. My husband expresses fear that "their" grandchildren will lose affection for him.

_____ 6. My husband feels that his divorce cheated his grandchildren of a "normal" grandparent relationship.

_____ 7. Our free time centers around "their" grandchildren.

_____ 8. "Their" grandchildren take advantage of my husband's need to please them.

_____ 9. I am excluded from plans when "their" grandchildren visit.

_____ 10. My husband does not insist that his grandchildren be respectful of me.

_____ Total

F R I E N D S

_____ 1. My husband's old friends seek out only his company.

_____ 2. I feel that at least two of "their" friends do not acknowledge our new marriage.

_____ 3. The wife of one of my husband's friends refuses to see me socially.

_____ 4. My husband's former wife is brought up in conversation in my company.

_____ 5. One of "their" friends reminds my husband that children from divorced homes have it rough.

_____ 6. I suspect that one of "their" friends carries back tales to my husband's ex-wife.

_____ 7. I feel merely tolerated by "their" friends.

_____ 8. One of "their" friends shows my husband photos of joint vacations from his past marriage.

_____ 9. "Their" friends quickly ask for my husband on the telephone after first greeting me.

_____ 10. The wife of one of my husband's friends tries to engage me in a conversation of a private nature in order to become "chummy."

_____ Total

_____   1. My husband looks at photos of himself and his ex-wife.

_____   2. My husband and I disagree over the disposal of such photos.

_____   3. My husband takes me to places frequented by him and his first wife.

_____   4. My husband compares our sex life with "theirs."

_____   5. Sex is a stressful issue.

_____   6. My husband makes negative comments comparing my spending habits to his ex-wife's.

_____   7. When we watch a show about divorce, my husband appears to become upset or anxious.

_____   8. My husband lets me know through words and/or facial expressions that certain songs and certain singers remind him of his first wife.

_____   9. When I want to talk about my feelings, communication comes to a halt.

_____   10. My husband openly criticizes me—alone, and in public.

_____   Total

_____ 1. I feel that my mother-in-law prefers my husband's ex to me.

_____ 2. My mother-in-law chastizes me.

_____ 3. My husband makes a point of describing the close relationship between his mother and former wife.

_____ 4. My mother-in-law hints that my husband remarried too quickly.

_____ 5. My mother-in-law feigns symptoms of serious illness when my husband doesn't call every night.

_____ 6. My mother-in-law says that our children are not as well behaved as "their" children.

_____ 7. My in-laws have secretive conversations in the corner when they visit.

_____ 8. My mother-in-law constantly brings meals over for us— unasked.

_____ 9. My husband admonishes me to be forgiving of his mother's harsh words to me, because "she won't be around forever!"

_____ 10. My mother-in-law seldom directly addresses me by name.

_____ Total

S C O R I N G

SECTION SCORE	CUMULATIVE SCORE	REMEDIAL ACTION
8–10	44–60	Professional help is needed immediately.
5–7	28–43	Serious problems prevail. Consider using behavioral methods to help yourself, as well as getting professional help.
3–5	11–27	Problems exist and should be addressed to improve your marriage.
0–2	0–10	Your "Second Wife" problems appear to be minimal and under control. The Progressive Muscle Relaxation Exercise would be a bonus in your life.

Help-Yourself Tools That Work

THIS CHAPTER OUTLINES
proven methods that you can use to initiate changes in yourself. It is
a fact that when you change your behavior, and look at things from a
slightly different perspective, others with whom you interact also
change. This phenomenon defines the very nature of change. In other
words, modifications of your actions and attitudes will cause a
"domino effect" on the actions and attitudes of others.

There are many behavioral methods for creating change. We will
present five of the most effective of these methods.

PROGRESSIVE MUSCLE RELAXATION EXERCISE

The Progressive Muscle Relaxation Exercise, which was developed by
Jenny Steinmetz, can effect a reduction in stress level. Stress reduction is an essential prerequisite for improving your marital relationship, due to the inner calm and control it bestows. An individual
who is calmly in control is able to respond rationally to potentially

volatile situations, whereas tense, overreactive individuals raise a conflict to the level of crisis. In order to create an optimal environment for inducing a "calm" state, select a quiet room with no distractions, wear comfortable clothing, and sit or recline so that all your muscles are supported. Read or memorize the instructions for the Progressive Muscle Relaxation Exercise (or record them in advance on a tape, and listen to the playback).

Follow each instruction carefully and completely. Don't skip any part of the body (unless injured), and don't skip any exercise. Also, make sure that you spend twice as much time relaxing a muscle as you do tensing that muscle.

Practice at least once daily for a minimum of ten days in order to condition (teach) yourself to respond to stress calmly. After that period of time, you may be conditioned sufficiently without going through the entire procedure. Simply take very deep breaths and slowly repeat the key words, "calm and relaxed," from the exercise. If you are unable to achieve complete relaxation, continued practice using the entire exercise may be needed. Do not be discouraged. You've been responding to stress in a particular way for many years. It takes patience to "unlearn" a "bad" response and to learn a "good" one.

Individuals with cardiac or breathing difficulties are advised to consult their physicians prior to undertaking this exercise.

Relaxation of the arms (four or five minutes)

Settle back as comfortably as you can and let yourself relax to the best of your ability.

Now, as you relax, clench your right fist.

Clench it tighter and tighter, and study the tension as you do so.

Keep it clenched and feel the tension in your right fist,
hand, and forearm.

Now relax . . .

Let the fingers of your right hand become loose . . .

Observe the contrast in your feelings.

Now, let yourself go and allow yourself to become
more relaxed all over.

Once more, clench your right fist really tight.

Hold it, and notice the tension again.

Now, let go, relax, and let your fingers straighten out . . .

Notice the difference once more.

Now repeat that with your left fist.

Clench your left fist while the rest of your body relaxes.

Clench that fist tighter and feel the tension.

And now relax . . . again, enjoy the contrast.

Repeat that once more, clench the left fist, tight and tense.

Now do the opposite of tension—relax and feel the difference . . .

Continue relaxing like that for awhile.

Clench both fists tighter and tighter, both fists tense, forearms tense.

Study the sensations . . . and relax . . .

Straighten out your fingers and feel that relaxation . . .

Continue relaxing your hands and forearms more and more.

Now bend your elbows and tense your biceps.

Tense them harder and study the tension feeling.

All right, straighten out your arms . . .

Let them relax and feel the difference again . . .

Let the relaxation develop.

Once more, tense your biceps.

Hold the tension and observe it carefully.

Straighten the arms and relax . . .

Relax to the best of your ability . . .

Each time pay close attention to your feelings
when you tense up and when you relax.

Now straighten your arms, straighten them so that you feel most
tension in the triceps muscles along the back of your arms.

Stretch your arms and feel the tension.

And now relax . . .

Get your arms back into a comfortable position . . .

Let the relaxation proceed on its own . . .

The arms should feel comfortably heavy as you allow them to relax.

Straighten the arms once more so that you feel
the tension in the triceps muscles.

Feel that tension . . . and relax.

Now let's concentrate on pure relaxation in
the arms without any tension . . .

Get your arms comfortable and let them relax further and further . . .

Continue relaxing your arms even further . . .

Even when your arms seem fully relaxed,
allow yourself to go that extra bit further . . .

Allow yourself to achieve deeper and deeper levels of relaxation.

Relaxation of the face, neck, shoulders, and upper back (four or five minutes)

Let all your muscles go loose and heavy.

Just settle back quietly and comfortably.

Wrinkle up your forehead now, wrinkle it tighter.

And now stop wrinkling up your forehead.

Relax and smooth it out . . .

Picture the entire forehead and scalp becoming smoother,
as the relaxation increases.

Now frown and crease your brows and study the tension.

Let go of the tension again . . .

Smooth out the forehead once more.

Now, close your eyes.

Keep your eyes closed, gently, comfortably, and notice the relaxation.

Now clench your jaws, push your teeth together.

Study the tension throughout the jaws.

Relax your jaws now . . .

Let your lips part slightly . . .

Appreciate the relaxation.

Now press your tongue hard against the roof of your mouth.

Look for the tension.

All right, let your tongue return to a comfortable
and relaxed position.

Now purse your lips, press your lips together tighter and tighter.

Relax the lips . . .

Notice the contrast between tension and relaxation . . .

Feel the relaxation all over your face, all over your forehead,
and scalp, eyes, jaws, lips, tongue, and throat . . .

The relaxation progresses further and further.

Now attend to your neck muscles.

Press your head back as far as it can go and
feel the tension in the neck.

Roll it to the right and feel the tension shift . . .

Now roll it to the left.

Straighten your head and bring it forward.

Press your chin against your chest.

Let your head return to a comfortable position and
study the relaxation . . .

Let the relaxation develop.

Shrug your shoulders right up.

Hold the tension.

Drop your shoulders and feel the relaxation . . .

Neck and shoulders relaxed.

Shrug your shoulders again and move them around.

Bring your shoulders up and forward and back.

Feel the tension in your shoulders and in your upper back.

Drop your shoulders once more and relax . . .

Let the relaxation spread deep into the shoulders
right into your back muscles.

Relax your neck and throat, and your jaws and other facial areas,
as the pure relaxation takes over and
grows deeper . . . and deeper . . . even deeper.

Relaxation of the chest, stomach, and lower back
(four or five minutes)

Relax your entire body to the best of your ability.

Feel that comfortable heaviness that accompanies relaxation.

Breathe easily and freely in and out . . .

Notice how the relaxation increases as you exhale . . .

As you breathe out, just feel that relaxation.

Now breathe right in and fill your lungs.

Inhale deeply and hold your breath.

Study the tension.

Now exhale, let the walls of your chest grow loose,
and push the air out automatically.

Continue relaxing and breathe freely and gently . . .

Feel the relaxation and enjoy it.

With the rest of your body as relaxed as possible,
fill your lungs again.

Breathe in deeply and hold it again.

Now breathe out and appreciate the relief,
just breathe normally . . .

Continue relaxing your chest and let the relaxation spread to your
back, shoulders, neck, and arms . . .

Merely let go and enjoy the relaxation.

Now let's pay attention to your abdominal muscles,
your stomach area.

Tighten your stomach muscles, make your abdomen hard.

Notice the tension.

And relax, let the muscles loosen and notice the contrast.

Once more, press and tighten your stomach muscles.

Hold the tension and study it.

And relax, notice the general well-being that
comes with relaxing your stomach.

Now draw your stomach in.

Pull the muscles right in and feel the tension this way.

Now relax again . . . let your stomach out . . .

Continue breathing normally and easily and feel
the gentle massaging action all over your chest and stomach.

Now pull your stomach in again and hold the tension.

Once more pull in and feel the tension.

Now relax your stomach fully . . .

Let the tension dissolve as the relaxation grows deeper.

Each time you breathe out, notice the rhythmic relaxation both in
your lungs and in your stomach . . .

Notice how your chest and your stomach relax more and more . . .

Let go of all contractions anywhere in your body.

Now direct your attention to your lower back.

Arch up your back, make your lower back quite hollow,
and feel the tension along your spine.

Now settle down comfortably again, relaxing the lower back.

Just arch your back up and feel the tensions as you do so.

Keep the rest of your body as relaxed as possible.

Localize the tension throughout your lower back area.

Relax once more, relaxing further and further . . .

Relax your lower back, relax your upper back, spread the relaxation
to your stomach, chest, shoulders, arms, and facial area . . .

These parts relaxing further and further and
further and even deeper.

Relaxation of the hips, thighs, and calves
(four or five minutes)

Let go of all tensions and relax.

Now flex your buttocks and thighs.

Flex your thighs by pressing down your heels as hard as you can.

Relax and notice the difference.

Straighten your knees and flex your thigh muscles again.

Hold the tension.

Relax your hips and thighs . . .

Allow the relaxation to proceed on its own.

Press your feet and toes downward, away from your face,
so that your calf muscles become tense.

Study that tension.

Relax your feet and calves.

This time, bend your feet toward your face so
that you feel tension along your shins.

Bring your toes right up.

Relax again . . . keep relaxing for awhile . . .

Now let yourself relax further all over . . .

Relax your feet, ankles, calves and shins,
knees, thighs, buttocks, and hips . . .

Feel the heaviness of your lower body as you relax still further.

Now spread the relaxation to your stomach, waist, and lower back.

Let go more and more deeply . . .

Make sure no tension has crept into your throat.

Relax your neck and your jaws and all your facial muscles.

Keep relaxing your whole body like that for awhile . . .

Let yourself relax.

Now you can become twice as relaxed as you are merely by taking in a really deep breath and slowly exhaling, with your eyes closed, so that you become less aware of objects and movements around you, and thus prevent any surface tensions from developing.

Breathe in deeply and feel yourself becoming heavier.

Take in a long, deep breath and exhale very slowly . . .

Feel how heavy and relaxed you have become.

In a state of perfect relaxation, you should feel unwilling to move a single muscle in your body.

Think about the effort that would be required to raise your right arm.

As you think about that, see if you can notice any tensions that might have crept into your shoulders and arm.

Now you decide not to lift the arm, but to continue relaxing . . .

Observe the relief and the disappearance of the tension.

Just carry on, relaxing like that . . . continue relaxing . . .

When you wish to get up, count backwards from four to one.

You should now feel fine and refreshed, wide-awake and calm.

Excerpted from Jenny Steinmetz, *Managing Stress before It Manages You* (Palo Alto, Calif.: Bull Publishing Co.), 20–27. Reprinted by permision of the publisher. Copyright © 1980 by Bull Publishing Co.

THOUGHT STOPPING

Thought Stopping, which was developed by Arnold A. Lazarus, is another behavior modification method that can be used to make changes in individuals. When a disturbing thought comes to mind, imagine a huge "Stop" sign and insert a pleasant thought, such as an image of your husband and yourself on a beach having a wonderful time. According to Lazarus, some people find it more effective to carry a small hand-shocking device and give themselves a "fairly unpleasant" electrical impulse upon saying "Stop!" Others find expletives such as "Go to Hell!" or "Get out of my head!" more effective than "Stop!"

See Arnold A. Lazarus, *Behavior Therapy and Beyond* (New York: McGraw-Hill, 1971; reprint, Jason Aronson, Northvale, N.J.: 1996).

VISUALIZATION

Visualization is a powerful and effective tool utilized in many areas of therapeutic change. It involves simply closing your eyes and imagining a scene that you wish to materialize. For example, envision your husband discarding his old photos—one by one—and lighting each one with a match. Concentrate on that image for a full fifteen minutes in a quiet, peaceful environment.

COMMUNICATION SKILLS

Many couples have inadequate communication skills. The following "problem solving" skill builder, which was developed by Neil Jacobson, Ph.D., can be used as a permanent step forward for you and your spouse.

All couples who live together over a long period of time face conflicts now and then. Even in an ideal marriage, periods of discord are inevitable. One of the hallmarks of a successful relationship is the ability to resolve these disputes in a way that is satisfactory to both parties.

Success at solving problems in your relationship means success in bringing about change. A relationship problem usually involves the desire for some kind of change on the part of at least one partner. . . .

Let us define problem solving as structured interaction between two people designed to resolve a particular dispute between them. Usually, but not always, the dispute is a complaint by one person concerning some aspect of the other's behavior. . . .

Problem Solving Setting

Problem solving is structured interaction. As such, it should only occur in certain settings and not in others. The first thing you and your partner need to do to get ready for problem solving is to set aside a time and a place in which discussions will be conducted. . . .

There should be an *agenda*. Ideally, the agenda will be planned in advance. Husband and wife should alternate the responsibility for planning an agenda. . . . Trying to resolve a grievance *when* the grievance occurs is usually ill-advised. When we are emotionally aroused, as we are bound to be when our partner behaves undesirably, we are not at our best; we are unlikely to problem solve in a rational manner. Discussing the issue at a neutral time, like during a prearranged problem solving session, makes it more likely that it will be dealt with effectively. . . .

Problem solving sessions should be relatively short. If one problem is being discussed, 30 minutes should be the maximum. You should allow no more than an hour for two problems. Never attempt the resolution of more than two problems in a single session. . . .

Problem Solving Attitude

The purpose of each and every problem solving session you have is to improve your relationship. Each time a relationship problem is solved, the relationship improves, and each partner becomes that much happier. It is in the interest of both partners to *collaborate* during these sessions. Each problem discussed, whether it be a gripe on the part of the woman or man, is a *mutual* problem. These two notions, that problem solving is *collaborative* and each problem discussed is a *mutual* problem, are absolutely critical. . . .

Since all potential marital problems have implications for both partners, every problem is a mutual problem. Collaboration is in the interest of both parties; therefore, each change agreed to by the partner will make his/her life more pleasant in the long run. Collaboration pays off, and for this reason it is the essence of problem solving. . . .

Problem Definition versus Problem Solution

A problem solving session has two distinct, nonoverlapping phases: a problem definition phase and a problem solution phase. During the problem definition phase, a clear specific statement of the problem is produced, a definition which is understood by both parties. . . . Then, during the solution phase, discussion is focused on generating and talking about possible solutions to the problem, and, finally, on the formation of an agreement designed to resolve the problem. . . .

Rule 1: In stating a problem, always begin with something positive. The way a problem is first stated sets the tone for the entire discussion. If you are about to say something which your partner might

---

interpret as critical, you want to make sure that you say it in a way that is least likely to result in him or her feeling angry. You want to maintain your partner's cooperation and collaborative spirit. Since it is difficult for all of us to accept criticism, since most of us immediately want to defend ourselves when we are criticized, and since we are likely to argue and counterattack when we are defensive, you must make every effort to minimize your partner's discomfort.

One very effective way of doing this is by beginning the statement of the problem with a positive remark, such as an expression of appreciation. To illustrate what we mean, below are lists of initial problem solving statements without and with positive beginnings.

WITHOUT A POSITIVE	WITH A POSITIVE
1. I feel rejected by you because you are seldom affectionate.	1. I like it when you hold me when we watch TV, but I feel rejected when you aren't affectionate in other situations.
2. Lately you haven't expressed much interest in hearing about my day.	2. I often look forward to coming home because I can unload all of my tensions on you by telling you what a rough day I had. I have always felt close to you at those times because you are such a good listener. But lately you haven't expressed much interest in hearing about my day.

If your partner is able to accept your criticism, s/he will remain in a collaborative spirit; otherwise, a counter-criticism or a statement of self defense is likely to follow. In this case, the problem solving session can quickly deteriorate. . . .

Rule 2: Be specific. When defining a problem, make sure that you describe the behavior of your partner that is bothering you. If you try hard enough you can almost always state your needs and your gripes in terms of specific words and actions. What is it exactly that your partner does or says that disturbs you or upsets you? Or, what would you like your partner to do in order to make you happier? The problem should be described in such a way that its presence or absence can be clearly determined by an observer. In other words, one should be able to either see it or hear it. Notice the contrast below between vague and specific problem definitions.

VAGUE	SPECIFIC
1. I get the feeling you aren't interested in what I do.	1. You seldom ask me questions about how my day was.
2. You don't want to sleep with me anymore.	2. Most of the time I initiate sex.

The key to understanding the feelings and reactions you have for your partner includes identifying his or her specific words and actions which bring out these feelings. Learning to pinpoint the relationship between behavior and feelings is an important skill in understanding a relationship.

Derogatory adjectives and nouns. One way to be vague in a problem formulation is to use derogatory labels as substitutions for descriptions of the behavior which bothers you. Consider the following examples:

1. You are inconsiderate.

2. You are lazy.

3. You are cold.

4. You are dogmatic and intolerant.

In none of these examples do we know what the accused partner had done to warrant these labels. The labels themselves are not only vague, they are provocative. . . .

If . . . your purpose is to maintain the other person's cooperation and keep communication clear and unambiguous, simply describe the behavior which displeases you and forget the labels. Consider the advantages of redefining the four examples listed above in terms of *behavior.*

1. When you fix yourself something to eat at night, you often neglect to ask me if I want something. (vs. "You are inconsiderate.")

2. Today you didn't make the bed, you left your dirty clothes on the floor, and you left used dishes in the living room. (vs. "You are lazy.")

3. In past months, you have seldom touched me except during sex. (vs. "You are cold.")

4. I've noticed that lately, when we discuss important decisions, you often interrupt me and insist upon your point of view. (vs. "You are dogmatic and intolerant.") . . .

Rule 3: Express your feelings. "I feel rejected and unloved when you don't include me in your Friday night plans."

"It's very frustrating to me when I want sex but have to wait for you to initiate it."

Almost always, when you find some aspect of your partner's behavior objectionable, it is because the behavior (or lack of it) leads you to become emotionally upset. . . . It is important to make these feelings known, in addition to pinpointing the behavior which led to the feelings. . . .

Rule 4: Be brief when defining problems. In general, the problem solving is oriented toward the future. The question which pervades most problem solving sessions is the following one: "something is troubling one of us; what can we do in the future to prevent a recurrence of this discomfort?" The only exception to this focus on the future is at the very beginning of the problem solving session, when the problem is defined. Since problem definitions describe behavior that upsets one or both partners, they must make reference to things that have occurred in the past. But the main objective in the problem solving definition phase is that the one who is not defining the problem understands exactly what it is that the partner is upset about and how s/he feels when the problem occurs. The definition should be as brief as possible. Once both partners have a clear understanding of what the problem is, the focus should immediately turn to "what do we do about it?"

Couples often become bogged down in this definition phase. They spend an excessive amount of time engaged in an unproductive focus on the past. This makes the probability of an argument higher . . . "Talking about" the problem may be interesting; but it is not problem solving. Don't confuse the two. . . .

Rule 5: Acknowledge your role in creating and maintaining the problem. This is the first of our rules which applies to the receiver of the problem definition as well as the one who has stated the problem. In the competitive disputes which all too commonly substitute for problem solving, each partner tries to deny the validity of the other's point of view or tries to cast blame on the partner. . . .

In a real problem solving session . . . both partners adopt the stance of admitting to their role in the problem rather than casting blame.

Wife: You spend very little time playing with Linda.

Husband: You're right, I don't spend a whole lot of time with her these days. (Admitting to his role).

Wife: I know that I can make it hard for you to play with Linda because I sometimes step in and interfere. (Admits to her role in the problem).

Notice that in this example both are admitting that they have some responsibility in creating the problem. Openly acknowledging your own role in contributing to the problem does wonders to change the spirit of the problem solving session from being very negative and blaming to being an open and honest, collaborative experience. . . .

General Rules

Before specifying the optimal strategies for generating good solutions to relationship problems, we will identify some general rules which should be observed during all phases of a problem solving session, whether the immediate task is one of problem definition or problem solution. These rules are equally applicable to both phases.

Rule 6: Discuss only one problem at a time. In a given problem solving session, only one problem should be discussed. When an additional problem is brought in, it is referred to as *side-tracking....*

Rule 7: Paraphrase. We are about to suggest a rule which may seem silly to you and a bit mechanical. First, from the beginning until the end of the problem solving session, every remark which your partner makes should be summarized by you before you respond. Second, after your summary statement, check its accuracy with your partner. If it was accurate, fine. Go ahead and give your response. If your partner does not think your summary statement was accurate, s/he should repeat the original remark, and you should try it again, until you both feel that the summary and the original are one and the same....

Rule 8: Don't make inferences. Talk only about what you can observe....

"As soon as I become more independent, you're going to leave me. That's why you're coming to therapy."

"You're trying to get me to do things that you *know* I shouldn't have to do for you."...

The above examples constitute attempts on the part of one spouse to speculate about what the partner is thinking or feeling. We refer to this practice as *mind-reading*. Problem solving is hindered by mind-reading. The entire process is built on being specific, and relying on what you can observe.

Rule 9: Be neutral rather than negative. When couples are fighting rather than collaborating, their interaction is frequently punctuated by attempts to put down, humiliate, or intimidate the partner. Such power struggles constitute the antithesis of problem solving. . . . The most prominent forms of verbal abuse that occur during arguments are put-downs, threats, and demands. All three categories share the function of removing the receiver of such a remark from a collaborative stance. . . . Instead of using threats or demands, simply describe the behavior that is upsetting you and the changes you would like to see.

Solving Problems and Forming Change Agreements

Rule 10: Focus on solutions. Once a couple has agreed on a definition to a problem, the focus should henceforth be on *solving* it. The discussion should be future oriented, and should answer the question, "what can we do to eliminate this problem and keep it from coming back?" . . .

The most effective way to maintain a focus on solutions and on the future is by *brainstorming*. This means the partners go back and forth, generating as many possible solutions to the problem as they can think of, *without regard to the quality of the solutions!*

Rule 11: Behavior change should include mutuality and compromise. In the spirit of collaboration and cooperation, whenever possible, problem solutions should involve change on the part of both partners.

This is even true in situations where the problem is clearly pointing to change on the part of one person. One reason for this is your partner is more likely to be willing to change if s/he isn't doing it alone. Another reason is that a partner can often help the other person change by providing feedback or teaching the partner some skill. In this sense, providing feedback or teaching a skill are the changes to which the second partner is agreeing. Finally, at times some behavior on your part may be serving as a reward for the behavior of your partner which you find undesirable or you may be able to do something following the change which you are asking for which will serve as a reward for that change.

For example, a couple was in conflict over who should do *what* with the kids. The wife wanted her husband to put the kids to bed at night. In the service of her own request, she granted him complete control over this task; she would leave him alone while he put the kids to bed. This was a big help, since in the past she often interfered with his efforts out of fear he would do something wrong. When she agreed to leave him alone, he unburdened her of this responsibility. . . .

Whenever you want to see a change in your partner, formulate the problem in two ways:

1. What do I ideally want?

2. What am I willing to settle for?

The answer to question #2 should be somewhat different from the answer to question #1. Otherwise, you haven't obeyed this principle. . . .

Rule 12: Discussing pros and cons of proposed solutions. Many couples find that a structured approach to discussing the possible solutions works best. It keeps them from escalating into arguments and serves to accomplish the task (solving the problem) efficiently. . . .

The format for discussing a proposal is to begin with the question, "If we are to adopt this solution, would it contribute to resolving the problem?" If the answer is "yes," they then discuss the costs of implementing that solution. Problem solving is usually a more positive experience if all of the good or potentially good things about the solution are discussed first before the costs are enumerated.

After the "costs" of a proposal have been discussed, you must decide whether to:

1. eliminate it from the list;

2. include it as part of your solution or change agreement; or

3. defer a final decision until you have completed discussion of all proposals. . . .

Whatever you decide to do with a given proposal, the process is repeated for each item on the list:

1. eliminate it if both agree that it is absurd;

2. decide whether it would contribute to solving the problem;

3. discuss the benefits of and costs to each spouse of adopting this proposal;

4. decide whether to eliminate, include, or defer.

Rule 13: Reaching agreement. Once brainstorming and related exercises have generated a series of possible solutions, the task becomes one of combining those solutions in such a way that change agreements are reached. Ultimately, the ability to agree on and implement behavior change is the acid test of effective problem-solving. . . . Keep in mind the following points:

A. *Final change agreements should be very specific.* They should be spelled out in clear, descriptive behavioral terms.

The agreement should clearly state what each spouse is going to do differently. . . .

Change agreements should not be open to interpretation. From the terms of the agreement, the behaviors that are required for compliance should be absolutely clear. The terms should include a description of the exact changes to be made, along with *when* these changes are expected to occur and, if possible, the frequency with which the new behaviors are to occur.

Here are some examples of bad agreements and the modifications that would be necessary in order to make them conform to this rule:

1. *Bad*—Jerry agrees to be home on time from now on.

   Good—On Monday through Friday, Jerry will be home by 6:30 P.M. If for some reason this is impossible on a particular night, he will let Marlene know by 4:30 P.M., and at that time will tell her when he will be home.

2. *Bad*—Mike will show more interest in Holly's day.

   Good—Each day when Holly and Mike get home, before dinner Holly will speak with Mike about the events of her day.

Mike will ask at least five questions of Holly regarding her day. He will also avoid the use of put-downs and other derogatory remarks, which to Holly imply disinterest.

You will note that these agreementa are quite structured in their content. They seem mechanical and artificial. Well, it is true that to some extent these kinds of agreements are mechanical and artificial. However, don't forget that you are in many cases trying to change very long-standing habits. Such habits are very difficult to change, and *the changes do not come naturally*. If the changes are to occur, a good deal of structure is necessary *at first*. Later, after the changes have been in occurrence for a while, they will become more natural and the need for such explicit structure is reduced. . . .

B. Final change agreements should include cues reminding each of you of the changes that you have agreed to make. In many instances, the problem is not that an individual is unwilling to comply with the partner's request, but when the time comes s/he simply forgets. . . .

C. Final change agreements should be in writing. . . . The written agreement, conveniently posted somewhere in the house, will remind you of what you have agreed to. . . .

Every agreement that is made should be reviewed at some specified future date to evaluate how well it is working and to determine whether it has successfully solved the problem. When you sign an agreement, set a date for this evaluation. Every agreement should have a "trial run" for a specified period of time.

Reviewing every agreement and renegotiating those that are not working constitute important steps in the process of conflict resolution.

Pride and Joy
The Lives and Passions of Women Without Children
AUTHOR: TERRI CASEY
$14.95, softcover

Pride and Joy is an enlightening collection of first-person interviews with twenty-five women who have decided not to have children. This book shatters the stereotypes that surround voluntarily childless women—that they are self-centered, immature, workaholic, unfeminine, materialistic, child-hating, cold, or neurotic. Diversity is a strong suit of the women profiled in this book. The narrators range in age from twenty-six-year-old Sarah Klein, who teaches second grade in an inner-city public school, to eighty-two-year-old Ruby Burton, a retired court reporter who grew up in a mining camp. The women talk about their family histories, intimate relationships, self-images, creative outlets, fears, ambitions, dreams, and connections to the next generation. Even though these women are not mothers, many voluntarily childless women help to raise and sometimes rescue the next generation while retaining the personal freedom they find so integral to their identities.

Forgiveness
The Greatest Healer of All

AUTHOR: GERALD G. JAMPOLSKY, M.D.; FOREWORD: NEALE DONALD WALSCH
$12.95, softcover

Forgiveness: The Greatest Healer of All is written in simple, down-to-earth language. It explains why so many of us find it difficult to forgive, and why holding on to grievances is really a decision to suffer. The book describes what causes us to be unforgiving and how our minds work to justify this. It goes on to point out the toxic side effects of being unforgiving and the havoc it can play on our bodies and on our lives. But above all, it leads us to the vast benefits of forgiving.

The author shares powerful stories, which open our hearts to the miracles that can take place when we truly believe that no one needs to be excluded from our love. Sprinkled throughout the book are Forgiveness Reminders that may be used as daily affirmations to support a new life, free of past grievances.

Create Your Own Love Story
The Art of Lasting Relationships

AUTHOR: DAVID W. MCMILLAN, PH.D.; FOREWORD: JOHN GRAY

$21.95, hardcover; $14.95, softcover

Create Your Own Love Story breaks new ground in the crowded and popular field of relationship self-help guides. *Create Your Own Love Story* is based on a four-part model—Spirit, Trust, Trade, and Art—derived from McMillan's twenty years of work in community theory and clinical psychology. Each of these four elements is covered in short, highly readable chapters that include both touching and hilarious examples from real marriages, brief exercises based on visualization and journal writing that are effective whether used by one or both partners, and dialogues that readers can have with themselves and/or their partners. This book shows readers how they can use their own energy and initiative, with McMillan's help, to make their marriage stronger, more enduring, and more soul-satisfying.

Love Sweeter Love
Creating Relationships of Simplicity and Spirit

AUTHOR: JANN MITCHELL; FOREWORD: SUSAN JEFFERS

$12.95, softcover

How do we find the time to nurture relationships with the people we love? By simplifying. *Love Sweeter Love* teaches you how to decide who and what is most important, how to work together as a couple, and how to savor life's sweetest moments. Mitchell has warm, practical, easy-to-understand advice for every-one—young, mature, single, married, or divorced—interested in creating sim-ple, sacred time for love.

Rites of Passage
Celebrating Life's Changes

AUTHORS: KATHLEEN WALL, PH.D., AND GARY FERGUSON

$12.95, softcover

Every major transition in our lives—be it marriage, high-school graduation, the death of a parent or spouse, or the last child leaving home—brings with it opportunities for growth and self-actualization, and for repositioning ourselves in the world. Personal ritual—the focus of *Rites of Passage*—allows us to use the energy held within the anxiety of change to nourish the new person that is forever struggling to be born. *Rites of Passage* begins by explaining to readers that human growth is not linear, as many of us assume, but rather occurs in a five-part cycle. After sharing the patterns of transition, the authors then show the reader how ritual can help them move through these specific life changes: work and career, intimate relationships, friends, divorce, changes within the family, adolescence, issues in the last half of life, and personal loss.

The Woman's Book of Dreams
Dreaming as a Spiritual Practice

AUTHOR: CONNIE COCKRELL KAPLAN; FOREWORD: JAMIE SAMS

$14.95, softcover

Dreams are the windows to your future and the catalysts to bringing the new and creative into your life. Understanding the power of dreaming helps you achieve your greatest potential with ease. *The Woman's Book of Dreams* emphasizes the uniqueness of women's dreaming and shows the reader how to dream with intention, clarity, and focus. This book will also teach you how to recognize the thirteen types of dreams, how your monthly cycles affect your dreaming, how the moon's position in the sky and its relationship to your astrological chart determine your dreaming, and how to track your dreams and create a personal map of your dreaming patterns. Connie Kaplan guides you through an ancient woman's group form called dream circle—a sacred space in which to regularly share dreams with others. Dream circle allows you to experience life's mystery by connecting with other dreamers.

The Woman's Book of Creativity

AUTHOR: C DIANE EALY, PH.D.

$12.95, softcover

The Woman's Book of Creativity supports women in their discovery of a life that is more joyful, spiritual, and—perhaps most obvious—abundantly creative. By inviting women to accept and nurture their own inherent ability to express their talents, author C Diane Ealy, Ph.D., offers guidance that can help to transform any woman's life from one of self-imposed limits to one of infinite freedom.

Healing Your Rift with God

A Guide to Spiritual Renewal and Ultimate Healing

AUTHOR: PAUL SIBCY

$14.95, softcover

God, says Paul Sibcy, is everything that is. All of us—faithful seekers or otherwise—have some area of confusion, hurt, or denial around this word, or our personal concept of God, that keeps us from a full expression of our spirituality. *Healing Your Rift with God* is a guidebook for finding our own personal rifts with God and healing them. Sibcy explains the nature of a spiritual rift, how this wound can impair our lives, and how such a wound may be healed by the earnest seeker, with or without help from a counselor or teacher. The book includes many personal stories from the author's life, teaching, and counseling work, and its warm narrative tone creates an intimate author–reader relationship that inspires the healing process.

TO ORDER OR TO REQUEST A CATALOG, CONTACT:

Beyond Words Publishing, Inc.

20827 N.W. Cornell Road, Suite 500

Hillsboro, OR 97124-9808

503-531-8700 or 1-800-284-9673

You can also visit our Web site at www.beyondword.com
or e-mail us at info@beyondword.com.

Beyond Words Publishing, Inc.

MISSION STATEMENT:

Inspire to Integrity

OUR DECLARED VALUES:

We give to all of life as life has given us.

We honor all relationships.

Trust and stewardship are integral to fulfilling dreams.

Collaboration is essential to create miracles.

Creativity and aesthetics nourish the soul.

Unlimited thinking is fundamental.

Living your passion is vital.

Joy and humor open our hearts to growth.

It is important to remind ourselves of love.